A Celebration of Yorkshire

A Celebration of Yorkshire

by
Barry Cockcroft

Dalesman Books
in association with
Yorkshire Television

The Dalesman Publishing Company Ltd.,
Clapham, Lancaster, LA2 8EB
First published 1989
© Tracestar Ltd 1989

Photographs (except pages 15, 42, 49, 51, 54, 57, 58, 88-top, 94 and 95).
© Stills, Yorkshire Television Ltd.

ISBN: 0 85206 977 4

The five books featured in *A Celebration of Yorkshire* were originally published as follows:-

Hannah in Yorkshire	1973
The Dale that Died	1975
The Ways of a Yorkshire Dale	1974
A Romany Summer	1979
Princes of the Plough	1978

Printed by Peter Fretwell & Sons Ltd.,
Goulbourne Street, Keighley, West Yorkshire BD21 1PZ

CONTENTS

Acknowledgements

I offer my grateful thanks to all those who gave freely of their time, recollections and talent to help me with this volume, particularly Brian Jeeves and Alan Harbour.

Since it was his idea to do it in the first place, I offer thanks to John Fairley.

Preface

IN THE early spring of 1968, a small and curiously assorted group of people assembled in a less than salubrious building in Burley Road, Leeds — used previously by a trouser manufacturer — and put up a sign.

It read: YORKSHIRE TELEVISION.

One of those pioneers was a former junior programme producer from Granada Television in Manchester who had crossed the Pennines intent on seizing the new opportunities in the Land of his Fathers — he could trace his Yorkshire ancestry back to Elizabeth 1st and beyond.

His name: Barry Cockcroft.

Cockcroft barely survived the next six chaotic, crisis-ridden and exhilerating months (several others did not) and was there when the fledgling took wing and the gold chevron of YTV fluttered forth unsteadily upon the region's television screen.

And almost immediately nose-dived towards oblivion.

Embarrassing problems with the complex machinery in the shiny new studios built alongside the trouser factory and an unfortunately timed strike presaged an event of cataclysmic proportions.

Yorkshire Television's very lifeline, the quarter mile high transmitter mast, collapsed spectacularly after being savaged by a Pennine storm. The screen went blank. The new station's managing director called everyone together and announced that bankruptcy would be, the inevitable consequence unless YTV could find some way of getting back on air very quickly indeed . . . . . .

Among the silent, stricken group listening to this was Barry Cockcroft. A journalist since leaving school, he had developed a passion for film making. And he knew precisely where he wanted to point a camera. Towards the virgin territory of rural Yorkshire.

Today, twenty-one years since those turbulent times, both Yorkshire Television and Barry Cockcroft have not only survived to tell their tale, but have told it to a receptive audience world wide.

YTV has acquired a global reputation *par excellence* for a wide sweep of programmes. But its multi-award winning documentary department is usually credited with creating the station's first major impact.

And Barry Cockcroft is the most senior of YTV's distinguished documentary makers. His own personal tally of awards and honours is formidable — they have been arriving regularly since 1972 — and he did not need to leave the white rose county to win them.

He specialised in presenting the Yorkshire region to the nation . . . . . . and then the rest of the world sat up and took notice, too. His programmes have been screened in many countries, from Scandinavia to Australasia, with conspicuous success.

It was, of course, towards the Yorkshire Dales and moorlands and the remarkable, stoic people who live and earn their living there that Cockcroft turned his gaze twenty-one years ago. His early films were confined to the region served by the station — and received with much enthusiasm. So he went looking for a subject which would establish his reputation on the entire ITV network.

And met Hannah Hauxwell.

Cockcroft readily acknowledges that it was an immense stroke of good fortune. There is only one Hannah. Today, she is a legend known to millions on several continents. Her magical film, *Too Long a Winter* aroused deep emotion wherever and whenever it was shown — it is believed that no documentary in the last quarter century has stirred such an explosive viewer response.

There followed what some grandly describe as Cockcroft's 'oeuvre' — a two decade celebration of Yorkshire and its unique personalities. A string of films down the years, accompanied by (since Cockcroft, from teenage days, has been what he calls 'a wordsmith') a series of books which told the full story . . . . added the vital extra dimension of the people and places featured in his films.

Hannah in Yorkshire was the first, a perennial best seller from the first day of publication in 1973. It has been described as 'a classic of Dales literature' and even J.B. Priestley was moved to bestow an accolade: 'Everybody who loves the Yorkshire Dales should acquire and cherish this book.'

It was followed by *The Ways of a Yorkshire Dale,* largely based on two more, hugely successful Cockcroft films. The first was *Sunley's Daughter,* a true and touching love story set in the North Yorkshire moorlands which enraptured and tore at the emotions of more than seven million viewers on the first of many showings.

The second, *Children of Eskdale,* won the kind of critical acclaim programme makers dream about. Nancy Banks Smith of the *Guardian,* most stylish of all television writers, declared it 'a classic', and it was granted an 'Honours Night' screening at the Prix Italia in Florence.

Even better, the viewing public was so affected by the simple, rural story of the Raw family and their five bonny, vibrant children — which concluded with hidden cameras recording the joy of the kids as they discovered the Palamino pony Dad had bought them instead of investing in a badly needed new tractor — that they campaigned for a repeat at a more suitable time for children. So it was networked again in the prime time Christmas programming of the same year.

Ways of a Yorkshire Dale presented the essential in-depth view of both *Sunley's Daughter* and *Children of Eskdale* and the book was further enhanced by stories of other dalesfolk Cockcroft had met or been told about during his years of research throughout Yorkshire.

Reader response was summed up by yet another Yorkshire luminary, Michael Parkinson, who declared: 'I warmly recommend *The Ways of a Yorkshire Dale* to all lovers of British life and tradition. Barry Cockcroft has a real gift for getting to the heart of Yorkshire and its people.'

The public had clearly developed an insatiable appetite for these poetic tales from the Dales and Yorkshire Television commissioned Cockcroft to keep them coming. He was more than happy to oblige.

So along came *The Dale that Died* an absorbing portrayal of a breathtakingly beautiful and virtually hidden valley in Upper Wensleydale, where ex-miner Joe Gibson was fighting a lone and valiant battle to maintain a tradition stretching back many centuries.

The book of the same name was a meticulous piece of research, building a fascinating evocation of an isolated Dales community long vanished, rich in detail, character and legend. The entire print sold out quickly and copies became collector's pieces.

Then came *A Romany Summer,* a result of Cockcroft's life-long interest in gipsies. At some

Barry Cockcroft, photographed with the Raw family of Eskdale (see pages 97–112).

physical risk he managed to spend a large part of one summer in the company of a genuine Romany, who wandered the lesser known byways of rural Yorkshire with his vardo, strangely assorted family — and more than thirty horses.

Cocker — he was christened Sir Montague Smith — made life very difficult for Cockcroft and his camera crew but a memorable film and a book of the same title was the result.

Another outstanding Yorkshireman whose life also pivots on horse power — the natural variety — is Geoffrey Morton. He has become internationally known as the champion of the Shire and other heavy horses. These magnificent beasts supplied the motive power for British agriculture for untold generations until the arrival of a generally affordable tractor launched a terrible slaughter.

But Geoff has traditionally spurned mechanical power on his windwhipped farm at Holme on

Spalding Moor and kept faith with the horse. Three documentaries have been made about Geoff and his docile giants. The first one, a short film shot in the early days of Yorkshire Television, was made, as you would expect, by Barry Cockcroft and shown in several regions because of its quality. And Cockcroft, naturally, wrote the book — *Princes of the Plough.*

Altogether, five books celebrating the romance of England's greatest county. And in this one volume, Barry Cockcroft has gathered together the essence of all five . . . a careful selection of outstanding literature to salute two major recent events in the vivid history of Yorkshire. The 21st anniversary of Yorkshire Television and the 50th anniversary of the *Dalesman* . . . *A Celebration of Yorkshire.*

Hannah in Yorkshire

Hannah Hauxwell

On the night of 30th January 1973 Hannah Bayles Tallentire Hauxwell appeared out of a landscape made sepia by a weakly setting winter sun. Dragging a white cow behind her as she bent against a driving blizzard, she entered four million, six hundred thousand homes.

Hannah Hauxwell was the central figure of a Yorkshire Television programme called 'Too Long A Winter', one of the most acclaimed documentaries of the last decade. The public response to the programme — or to be more exact, the response to the life and personality of Hannah — was phenomenal.

YOU could pass through Baldersdale a thousand times and never catch a glimpse of Hannah Hauxwell. Her home is set by a lonely stretch of the Pennine Way and only once a month does she follow the path of the tired, straggling hikers up the fields one and a half miles to the road at the top of the dale. Her brief contact with the world outside Low Birk Hatt Farm, where life has not changed for many generations, occurs when she lifts a cardboard carton perched on the dry-stone wall by the road. It is left there each month, and has been for many years, by the grocer at Cotherstone, one of the attractive villages dotted along the road through Teesdale as it leaves Barnard Castle and winds up to County Durham.

Hannah's monthly food bill with the grocer has crept up to just over £5 these days. She has had to 'put the brake on' (one of her favourite expressions). It allows only for butter, eggs, sugar, lard, margarine, onions, tomatoes, bread, one tin of Spam and a large lump of cheese to give her the protein the doctor has warned she must have. That is not much, by any standards. But it is all she can afford on her income, which can amount to £280 a year if things go well. A little over £5 a week, and there are expenses to come out of that.

When she arrives back home with the groceries there is rarely time for Hannah to sit down and get her breath back. The calf, Septimus, always needs her and it is usually time to milk Her Ladyship, her beloved white cow. This means a chase round the pasture with a pail and three-legged stool, and feeding Septimus involves a journey with a bucket down to her only source of water, the stream which flows fifty yards from her front door and which she shares with the cattle of the surrounding pasture. Low Birk Hatt has never had running water or electricity. It is so isolated that in winter Hannah frequently goes for more than ten days without seeing another human being. She has no man and all her close relatives are dead.

At the age of fifty-one she has a gleaming halo of pensioner's white hair which sprays around a face so smooth, creamy and clear that it could be a child's. Her thin, sinewy body is clothed with intricate and seemingly never-ending layers of well-laundered rags. She speaks with a slow and touching courtesy which belongs to another age. She is probably the most vulnerable and

13

materially deprived person in the British Isles. She is probably the most content.

Hannah Hauxwell's life of serene deprivation seems to have been ordained. It reaches back to the time she was born in 1927. Life was relentlessly hard for the ordinary folk in the Yorkshire Dales when Hannah was a child. Mechanization in the shape of tractors, harvesters and hay mowers had scarcely touched this land which traditionally accepts new technology a decade or more after most farming communities. So the work on Low Birk Hatt Farm, Baldersdale, was accomplished by sweat. Long, lonely hours and sweat.

For Hannah nothing has changed since her childhood. Indeed the Hauxwells have borne this burden with an equanimity which reaches back for generations. They were always raised to a life of constant physical hardship and expected nothing else. But there was a new harshness in the lifestyle of the Hauxwell's during the childhood of Hannah. The country was on the rack of the Depression, and the working class had faced up to the last famine it was prepared to tolerate. The men of Jarrow had been on the march, a file of gaunt faces which passed silently by, just fifteen miles from the fields where Hannah's father scythed the long grass and twice a day milked his cows by hand. William Bayles Hauxwell, fighting his eighty sparse acres, knew little of this drama taking place just over the hills. Dales' farmers never did have much time to spare for affairs outside their own self-contained environment. Forty years ago the boundaries of their world were limited on the one side by the markets where they bought and sold their animals, and on the other by the heights of the common grazing land where their sheep scratched a living. This insular attitude is emphasised in Baldersdale because it is a closed dale. The road just peters out on the moors at its head, and the only non-residents who travel it regularly are the men who tend the reservoirs which stretch past Low Birk Hatt.

Hannah's first memories of her father go back to happier times when he would bring back small presents for his only child whenever he visited Barnard Castle, twelve miles down the narrow lanes of Teesdale. 'He never forgot to bring me something back — usually buns from a shop called Guy's. But the treats stopped when the hard times came. I don't know how he managed, the prices were so bad.'

Most farmers in the dales go to market less than a dozen times a year, to sell their fatstock or buy new blood for their herds and flocks at those atmospheric, corrugated iron and concrete auction rings where the weekly rituals of rural business life are conducted to this day. When they do, it is a life and death matter. Even now a bad day at market can prejudice the life and plans of a family for half a year. For a long spell during the thirties every market day was bad.

The Hauxwells had an extra burden. Most farming families care for one, or perhaps two, of their old folk. But William and Lydia Hauxwell shared the dwindling comfort of their farm with four ageing relatives — William's parents and two elderly uncles. The farmhouse which stands on the lip of Hury reservoir is an empty and echoing place today, now that only Hannah is left, but forty years ago it was full to the brim. Seven mouths to feed, money scarcer than it had ever been and only one able-bodied man. It is not difficult to understand why Hannah's mother and father decided not to add any more children to their family, but this meant that Hannah was deprived of the companionship of brothers and sisters. As a child, Hannah may not have gone hungry like her contemporaries in the slum terraces of the cities, since farms always have eggs and the odd hen which has outlived its usefulness, but the city children at least had the comfort of playmates and games which could help them to forget their environment.

For a time Hannah did have one small friend at the next farm down the valley, which today stands empty and crumbling like so many others in the more remote dales, where communications are poor and the land only good for grazing.

Top, left: Hannah's mother, Lydia Hauxwell.
Bottom, left: Hannah Hauxwell, aged ten.
Right: Hannah as a young woman.

Hanging out washing at the back of Low Birk Hatt Farm.

'Yes, I had Derek for a playmate when I was very young. Derek Brown from Blackton, just a little way across the valley. His mother was my father's cousin and he used to come for "Hannah girl" as he called me, so that he could walk with me to school. But he and his family left quite soon, before I was ten, and there was never anyone else.

'Those days were quite miserable because Father was doing so badly at market, just like everyone else. He used to come home depressed because he had paid a high price for the farm — £1,600 — and the mortgage payments were very heavy. I once saw some of the papers he left behind with the details of his income and expenditure, and I just don't know how he managed.'

'I was too young to understand properly what was going on at the time. Anyway I was busy playing around in the fields with the animals and helping to feed them. I remember we had a grand little horse called Dick — a faithful, honest horse who I used to ride occasionally. I liked it best when he used to drag a sledge like a big strong gate and I was allowed to ride on it. We had dogs too, but I wasn't allowed to play with them because they were working dogs. Except one, an old English sheepdog called Roy. He used to have fits so it didn't matter me playing with him. I think I used to spoil him. As for toys, I didn't have many but that's understandable. I do recall a little rabbit someone gave me. It wasn't made in the lovely materials you have now but it was nice and soft. Now, I treasured that but it vanished rather strangely around the time that little Derek left. I'm not making any accusations but I always wondered.'

As Hannah played innocently in the farmyard, a real tragedy was developing in the Hauxwell household. Her father became ill with pernicious anaemia and the doctor announced that he would never again be a completely fit man. He was told to take care of himself and to reduce his workload, but of course he didn't — he couldn't. There was quite a sleeping problem in the house which only had three bedrooms. One uncle had to bed down in the space under the stairs, and Hannah slept in the same bed as her mother and father.

'It was a big blue bed and we all three used to sleep in that. But I remember one morning when I woke up and realised that something was different. I was in another bed in the room, all by myself and wrapped up in a soft green eiderdown. The I saw something I'll never forget. I can picture it now. The door was open and the undertaker, all dressed in black, was standing there at the top of the stairs. You see, my father had died during the night and they'd moved me. It seems he'd been taken ill with pneumonia and he just died. He was only thirty-seven.'

'I don't recall the funeral — they kept me away from that. Miss Leach, an old friend of the family, came to look after me the day they buried him at Romaldkirk. I didn't get to know my father well because I was too young when he was alive, but I think he must have been a grand man. One of my regrets is that I don't have a photograph of him as an adult. Mother wanted one taken when they got married but he said he wouldn't bother. It cost money. But I do know that Father had many plans for us had he lived.'

Hannah's mother was left a widow with a child, a mortgaged farm and four old people to care for. This desperate situation was relieved by the arrival of Hannah's uncle, who was glad to come and manage the farm since the living on his own had become even more precarious than that at Low Birk Hatt. Hannah found the new member of the family a difficult person because he had marital problems and was subject to fits of depression. Unfortunately she could draw little comfort from her schooldays.

'No, I didn't like school at all. I didn't regret leaving when I was fourteen and never have to this day. I liked the under-teacher, Miss Walker, very much and I cried when she left, which was quite a bit before the war. The head teacher was a kind woman in her way and she would buy apples, oranges and sweets for us out of her own pocket at times like Whitsuntide and Christmas.

But she and I just didn't get on. It's not that I was a naughty girl, I was just very shy, and maybe not the quickest to pick things up. Anything I could manage I did, such as reading or spelling, but arithmetic — well! She was the sort of person, you know, who had her favourites and I wasn't the only one to become at variance with her. I always remember one day she was being cross with one of the less fortunates, and comparing him with a boy called Maurice who was a favourite. She snapped "Yes! Maurice has a mother," as though the other poor boy was like the character in Uncle Tom's Cabin who wasn't born. He just growed and hadn't had a mother. I don't think really those were my happiest days.'

Hannah's relationship with her mother was the one warm, complete and stable bond of her life. Lydia Sayer Hauxwell brought into Low Birk Hatt accomplishments which were uncommon, to say the least, in the bleak and basic life of Baldersdale. Her education and upbringing had embraced music and literature. She was a talented musician and her dowry included a small, foot-powered organ which still stands in the kitchen of Low Birk Hatt, and is played occasionally by Hannah who inherited her mother's love of music.

'Mother's mother was a lady who, I think, was born in good circumstances and brought up at the Manor House at Bowes. The family owned hotels in the area, and Mother had acquired tastes and traits through them. I remember she used to make up satin dresses for her sisters and she had received a share of good jewellery. Mother was so wonderful, I'm sorry to say I'll never be the woman she was. I don't even look like her. She was little and plump and she would sing and play the organ — and laugh. You know, when one is young one doesn't think, but in these later years I've thought a lot and come to understand just what a wonderful person she was, that having her life she could still laugh. She had to go out and work on the farm and, at the same time, nurse the elderly people who were all poorly in turn. The last to go was Grandma Elizabeth who died in 1940. We raised sheep and cattle and we all had our jobs, particularly at haymaking and sheep-shearing time. I was never much good at sheep-shearing.

'Mother and I had a lot of happiness together and I do wish we had enjoyed better circumstances. But she used to keep everyone's spirits up. We were very close. I used to hear girls at school saying that they wouldn't or couldn't tell their mothers various things, but there was nothing I couldn't and didn't tell her. We shared everything — the beauty of the countryside, the books and the music.'

The other influence in Hannah's childhood was her grand-father, James Hauxwell. He had arrived in Baldersdale one day towards the end of the nineteenth century. A dashing figure with a shovel in his hand and a poem or recitation for any occasion on his lips, James Hauxwell stood out among the navvies digging the long and winding Hury Reservoir, which banks up to the front garden of Low Birk Hatt. His home was 'up country', at a farm called Swinelayers in Manfield, between Piercebridge and Darlington, but he was a travelled man and had served with the army in India. He could quote from Kipling and other popular Victorian authors, a social attribute which gave him a decided advantage when he came to court Grandma, herself a well-read young lady. They had one other thing in common — the memory of genteel backgrounds. James's father was reputed to have been cheated out of his inheritance by an elder brother when their wealthy father died.

The memory of her grandfather still makes Hannah laugh. 'I think maybe he was a harum scarum,' she says delightedly. 'I suppose drink was his fault, to a fault. But oh, how he could recite. Listening to Granda' reciting as he sat in his chair by the fire, is one of the things I remember best from my childhood. He could quote from *Bell's Elocutionist:* "Balshazzars Feast" and the "Arabs Farewell to his Steed" and many more. It was lovely.'

Collecting drinking water from the stream fifty yards from the farm.

Apart from Grandad James, the elder Hauxwells did not have much time to spend amusing Hannah, but when she grew old enough to wander further afield she spent a lot of time with a happy and warmhearted family at Clove Lodge, a farm perched on a hill on the other side of the reservoir. There was still no child of Hannah's age for her to play with, but she was made welcome.

'There was Mr. and Mrs. Atkinson and their son Douglas, who was ten years older than me, and Mrs. Atkinson's two sisters, the Misses Elizabeth and Annabella Hind. After my father died I generally used to go to them for Christmas, and stop a few days.

I can still remember the Christmasses at home before Father died. I used to hang up my stocking and there would be an apple, an orange, a few sweets and nuts, a bit of coal and an onion popped inside. Once I got a dolly, but that was a special Christmas. They made quite a thing of Christmas at Clove Lodge and I loved it. They used to get a juniper tree from the hillside and put it in the middle of an old cart-wheel and we'd all gather round and decorate it with tinsel and things. There was always a present for me. I remember Mrs. Atkinson gave me a brush and comb one year, and when I arrived another year Miss Elizabeth was just finishing off a little black and brown apron for me. Then they would light the fire in the east room and there would be a chicken and a plum pudding on the table. They were so kind and always encouraging me to come and visit. The only time I ever played cards and dominoes was when I stayed with them. I used to sleep on their sofa, by the window. Mind you, they had their problems because Miss Annabella took fits and I used to help look after her sometimes.

'Christmas at Clove Lodge was always something to look forward to. In later years when I was a teenager living with Mother and Uncle, we never had what most people would call a proper Christmas. Mother and I would always go to chapel of course, and sometimes we would have a chicken. Otherwise it was just a normal day with no exchanging of presents or anything like that.'

Chapel was a strong influence in Baldersdale at that time. Today Hannah's personal library reflects the devout attitudes of the elder Hauxwells and consists largely of Bibles — sixteen at the last count — and books on theology. The Sundays of Hannah's young life were devoted to worship, and her spiritual values remain unchanged although she seldom has the opportunity of attending services these days.

'Actually we were mixed up with both church and chapel. I used to go to the church Sunday school and then to the church service afterwards. Mother and Grandma used to come to the church service and then we'd go on to the Methodist chapel in the evening. Grandma was church and Mother was chapel, you see, so we patronised both. But I was baptised into the church.

'It was through the Sunday school that I managed to get out of the dale a bit. We used to go on coach trips to places like Redcar, Morecambe and the Lakes. The longest trip we ever had was to Loch Lomond. The coach picked us up at the top of the road at six o'clock in the morning and brought us back in the small hours. That's still the farthest I've ever been away from home.'

As she grew into womanhood, Hannah was expected to take a full share in the work of the farm. Although the war had given farm prices a much-needed boost, money was still not plentiful. Uncle had to be paid a good wage since he was managing the farm and supporting his wife and family, from whom he was parted. He was also hot-tempered.

I'm afraid I did have some unpleasantness with Uncle. You see I've never been too quick at things — in fact it takes me a long time to do anything — and he would become impatient. There were bad patches. I understand now it was because he had these other stresses. His wife used to come sometimes to see him and that was never a very happy time. But he could be a jolly man sometimes and I was rather fond of him and did my best to please him. I used to help with the haymaking, following the mower round because the cutterboard dragged the grass instead of letting it lie in swathes. It was often my job to catch the horses and bring in manure and hay with the cart. Those horses were a handful and once I sprained my wrist rather badly trying to control them.

'But through all these times my mother was wonderful and I wished we could go away and live quietly together, without all the worries. We did own an old derelict house on a little piece of land farther down along Hury reservoir. I understand Father was planning to repair it one day, but we were never able to do anything about it and once had to sell some of the land to help things along. Mother was everything to me and even when she was in good health I'd wake up in the night and worry about what I would do without her. It was an awful time when she did become poorly. One summer she went to the doctor who sent her to hospital for X-rays, but they didn't seem to be able to help. At the back end of the year we had that dreadful Asian 'flu epidemic and we all caught it, only Mother never really picked up. She was just so weak and it got worse and worse, and then I got this feeling . . .

'I used to cry during the night and during the day when she couldn't see me. But I did stop myself when I had to go upstairs to take her food and the things that she needed. I thought it was something I'd never be able to hide, but I managed. Both Uncle and I became very worried and I remember him coming to me one night after he'd been to see her and saying "By . . . she looks far worse than I ever thought she was." Then one Tuesday when I was out working she developed a bad pain, so I went up to one of the neighbours who had a telephone and they rang the doctor. An ambulance was sent and she became worse and worse as we were getting her ready. She died on the way to hospital. One has never ceased to miss her.'

It is fifteen years since her mother's death but Hannah still feels the pain as though it was yesterday. She cannot hide the tears and cannot even speak about the funeral. Lydia Hauxwell, the happy little plump woman who could still laugh despite the crushing blows dealt out by fate, was buried alongside the young husband she lost almost a quarter of a century before.

Poor, miserable Hannah now had no one to turn to for comfort. Her uncle had always been preoccupied with his own worries and his health also began to fail.

'I had quite a time with him. Mother was a good patient, of course, but I'm afraid that he wasn't. He wanted attention all the time and I had the farm to look after. They said he had rheumatism but I realised that it was more than that because he worsened rapidly. He was so bad that I even had to go and get a neighbour to help me get him up. Then the doctor said he'd better go into hospital in Barnard Castle. I was sorry in a way but he wasn't happy with the attention I could give him. I'm afraid he died there. I don't know now whether I should have stuck it out with him but the doctor insisted that he ought to go into hospital. I was really very fond of him, you know.'

And so Hannah found herself totally alone. She had little knowledge of the outside world and was not in any way equipped to go out and meet it on equal terms. Just once a year she has to make a business visit to the pleasant little market-town of Barnard Castle. The event always unsettles her for days. But otherwise she rarely leaves her dale — in fact rarely leaves Low Birk Hatt, except for those monthly trips to the wall by the road for her groceries. It would be a desolate life for most people but Hannah is radiantly content.

'You see, I can't see myself anywhere else or in any other position. I'm so attached to the homestead because only our family has lived in this house since it was built.

'One is free, and the lovely countryside has a strong appeal for me. It has such continuity and

Hannah, dressed in intricate and seemingly never-ending layers of well-laundered rags. She reared a beast to go to market once a year.

it'll be here for a long time yet, unless man gets too clever for himself and blows it all up. When I've been on my favourite walk down by the side of the reservoir, I've often stopped to think. I've looked around and said to myself "Well, if I haven't got money in my pocket that's one thing nobody can rob me of. It's mine . . . mine for the taking." You see, I'm not cut out to be in any other place. I have no ability, I'm not even a good farmer because you can't be on a shoestring. Anyway I couldn't manage to farm what I call properly, doing the haymaking and looking after a great lot of cattle. The few I keep are about what I can cope with. I have rather a love-hate relationship with them as it is, but I must say I'm very attached to my old white cow — Her Ladyship I call her — and the calf Septimus.

'When Uncle died I decided to sell all the cattle because I was unable to care for them. Mr Tom Addison, the auctioneer, was very good and a few neighbours came to help get things ready. But it wasn't a happy day and I never went outside. I was left with about twenty bullocks and some good stirks but I was very unlucky with the prices and there was only about £500 to come back at the end of it all. Apparently the market for cattle wasn't good at the time, and I was told later that if I'd waited for another month I would have made another £4 or £5 a head. It was a bad do, and it sort of put a damper on everything.

'I've never been a business woman and I don't like handling money. I generally rear a beast to go to market once a year. Little Septimus will be the next but my friend Mr Atkinson at Clove Lodge takes it to auction for me. I wouldn't be a ha'porth of use at market with all those men — well, some of them are rough.'

Middleton-in-Teesdale auction mart is certainly no place for a maiden-lady with Hannah's sensitivities. When her beast is carried off she waits nervously at home for the result because although the auctioneer only takes about two and a half minutes to dispose of the animal, it is a vital time for Hannah and yields more than a third of her astonishingly low income.

'It varies a little, of course, but I have to manage on around £280 a year. The last beast I sold, he made £108 but there were expenses to come out of that — transport and so forth. I also take a few cattle in for neighbouring farms. I look after them and graze them on my land, which brings in somewhere around £160. On top of all that I get a subsidy of around £23 for Her Ladyship and another of £10 or £11 for the calf. Out of that I have to buy the meal — that's a fairly big thing — and pay a man to do the hay-timing. Coal is rather an expensive item — over £30 a year, but I like a fire. It's one thing I've never economised on because a good fire is essential here. But it's necessary to economise on most items. I have a system of keeping expenditure down to the very bare necessities. In some respects I would say that I can't even afford some necessities so I keep it down to the bare essentials. I put the brake on and keep it on — it's the only way.'

Hannah may not have much of a farm in terms of stock and produce but she works it completely alone, and with her bare hands. She does not even own a wheelbarrow.

'I suppose I do have to be the farmer and the farmer's wife. But I've gone outside and roughed about ever since I was twelve. I've even carried sacks of coal on my back from the top road when I've been cut off by a snow storm. There are quite a few jobs I find hard to do though, like repairing gaps in the dry-stone walls. I can manage the smaller stones all right but I often come across great big stones which I can't lift. The property, of course, is quite a headache because it's always in need of repairs, but I just carry on and do my best.

'Winter brings all sorts of problems. I have to get all my water from the stream and when it freezes I have to take a pick to it and melt the ice in the house. When there's a long spell of dry weather the stream dries up so I have to go and look for water somewhere else. Having a bath is a bit of a problem. I boil the kettle on the Calor gas stove two or three times and I do my best to have my bath in a cowpail by the fire. It's not a fast job. If I admitted the truth, I would say I don't have a bath as often as I ought but I do like one if a friend is going to call.

'Sometimes I feel I've missed a patch out of my life, missed being a woman you might say. I've never bothered with lipstick and powder but I do like clothes. I know I live in these old rags but I do that because the cattle are no respecters of clothes. My best clothes are nothing special, of course, and I only wear them on the few occasions I go out. I have a nice blue dress someone very kindly gave me. But I'm not a glamour girl, I don't think, and I haven't much money to spare for buying clothes. The last new dress I bought was a black one, when my mother died. But friends have been kind in giving me clothes and I don't really want for them.'

Hannah's isolation and gentle introversion meant that she didn't meet many eligible young men. Much of her young womanhood was spent in the company of older people, but she has thought about marriage.

'Yes, of course, one does think. But it takes two to have an opinion of that kind — you can't just walk into a shop and say "I want a husband". When I was younger there were people I liked but there was no one really special in that line. I suppose I'm very much like the spinster lady who went to her clergyman and complained about the lack of a husband. He told her she must leave it in the Lord's hands, to which she replied "That's all very well, but up to now the Lord's made badly out!" Marriage is a wonderful thing if one is privileged to meet the right person and it turns out well. But it must be one of the worst things in the world to have to share a home and life with someone that you become utterly at variance with.'

The loneliness and the unremitting harshness of Hannah's life, aggravated by her sparse diet, brought her to a low ebb when she was forty.

'I think I got rather down in myself. I'd been going to see the doctor for quite a while and he thought I wasn't improving very much, so he suggested I went to hospital. A neighbour very kindly agreed to look after my animals and I stayed there for eight weeks. It was the first and only occasion I've spent any length of time away from Low Birk Hatt. I was very happy there. I went a stranger and came away with one or two friends. I saw television for the first time and found it very interesting. Of course there was nothing seriously wrong with me. I'm afraid I took it rather badly when I came back. I gradually got used to the same thing again but oh, it wasn't the same when I came home at first. It seemed very quiet, and no one to talk to.'

There is a real risk that Hannah may fall ill again one day and be unable to call for help. She would have to wait for the postman to find her, or some neighbour to notice that her oil lamp had not been lit for some time. Hannah says 'It's a chance I'll just have to take.'

When she has time to relax Hannah likes to read and listen to her battery radio, which was given to her by one of a small but devoted network of friends, nearly all of whom live at least 100 miles away from Baldersdale. They met Hannah as they rambled along the Pennine Way and were moved by her nun-like tranquillity and happy acceptance of her spartan life. They write and send her birthday cards and books. Unfortunately, long hours of reading by a flickering oil lamp have affected Hannah's eyesight and she has to ration this pleasure.

'The radio is a great friend of mine. I like to hear the man saying "This is the World at One" and I do enjoy "The Archers". The other night I had a real treat. I listened to "Grand Hotel", the Salvation Army Singers, the "Hebrew Slaves Chorus" and Elizabeth Schwarzkopf singing "Don't be Cross". It was really grand, and all of a slap on the same night.

'Probably my favourite book is *Little Women*. A dear little lady across the dale sent it to me many years ago. It was the first book I ever read. There are lots of books I'd like to read but I have to be careful with my eyes these days. They ache so much. Poetry about the dales I also like

Reading by oil lamp — until recent times the only form of lighting at Low Birk Hatt Farm.

very much. We had poets in Teesdale, you know — Richard Watson and William Langstaff. I particularly like some lines from Mr Langstaff, who wrote:

> Long, silent hills,
> Clear, singing streams.
> Among them, we're close to God.

'Those lines appeal to me very much because well — they're my life. That's the picture I see every day, and never tire of it. From my window one can see the hills and the trees, and then there's Hunder Beck which runs down by the side of the house. On still summer nights it sings songs to me.'

There is something inspirational about Hannah which affects everyone who meets her. She is really of another age and another world, with a quite different set of values. Her spiritual repose, infinite trust and tranquil, uncomplaining acceptance of a way of life which is unacceptable by modern standards make her a unique person. This quality is so powerful that it does not diminish when processed by the media and projected from a television screen.

Hannah realises that her enclosed world is really incompatible with the one we know (the one she dislikes and distrusts) and that advancing years and ill health will finally force her away from her beloved home in a hidden corner of a half-forgotten dale. There has been nothing in her life up to now to prepare her for such a change. It will be like hauling someone out of the middle of the nineteenth century.

'I don't know what's the best to do. I like the house and I'd like to keep it — it's home. I think I must be a Wilkins Micawber; I'm waiting for something to turn up, maybe. Honestly, in my own mind I don't know what to do. The time will come when ill health — rheumatism maybe — or circumstances will make me consider changing my life.

'But I love it here, so the old house and me, we'll stay together for as long as we can.'

Hannah Revisited

THE progress of Hannah Baynes Tallentire Hauxwell during the sixteen years since the making of 'Too Long a Winter' has been remarkable by any standards. Public interest and the attention of the media, continues unabated to this day. The path down to Low Birk Hatt Farm has never been so well worn as hundreds, nay thousands, of people have scrambled over the stiles and ploughed through the mud to pay homage to Hannah. They bring gifts, take photographs, demand autographs, and generally act as though they are in the presence of minor royalty.

Hannah Hauxwell is undisputedly the First Lady of the Yorkshire Dales, and she is known throughout most of the English speaking world. That documentary which established her so permanently in the affections of the British public harvested an impressive array of awards and was distributed to many countries, from Europe to North America, and Australasia. Their response to the inspirational force of Hannah was equally strong. People travelled from all over Europe to find her. One family of Scandinavians even turned up at Low Birk Hatt on her birthday — with presents and cards; numberless gifts arrived from places farther afield, including a whole cheese sent overland from New Zealand, causing confusion at many post offices and a log jam in the front room of that far-away farmhouse in the High Pennines. Perhaps the most confused man of that particular period in the continually evolving story of Hannah was a Dutch television executive. His station innocently transmitted 'Too Long A Winter' one night, and a couple of days later he had difficulty getting through the entrance hall of his studios. It was full of presents for Hannah sent by viewers. In bewilderment (it seems he had not seen the programme himself) he rang up Yorkshire Television in Leeds and uttered some long remembered words, spoken in a heavy Dutch accent — 'Who the Hell is Hannah Hauxwell!'

Who, indeed, is Hannah Hauxwell? No one has been able to satisfactorily analyse the power of this deliberately spoken, white-haired lady. What quality within her moves people of all kinds and callings so deeply — indeed moves some to amazing acts of devotion. One man, an ordinary wage earner, was so affected by the programme, and a pilgrimage to meet Hannah face to face, that he set about raising a very large sum of money for a very particular purpose. He launched a campaign of such passion and energy among his workmates at a large chemical works in Lancashire that, with a little help from the somewhat wide-eyed management of Yorkshire Television, he swiftly acquired sufficient to pay men to spill their sweat and bring the boon of electricity to Low Birk Hatt Farm. The ground was so unyielding as they neared Hannah's house that the exhausted men from the North Eastern Electricity Board had to use explosives to plant the poles carrying the lines. As they finished their work, a team of volunteers, raised and led by this remarkable man, wired Hannah's place from top to bottom and installed a cooker and a television set.

The great switch-on was a moment to savour, with Hannah's smile out-shining the new light fittings, and was duly recorded on film. And the person who conceived it all, and brought it about, quietly faded into the background. A most remarkable man.

Naturally, the story of electricity arriving at Low Birk Hatt made page leads in every national newspaper. But then, it only takes a couple of inches of snow in Leeds for every news editor to despatch a team to write up another story about the way Hannah is coping with yet another winter. And why not? Public demand for news about Hannah is insatiable.

Hannah's rise to her present position has been steady but inexorable. Other characters brought to national notice by the media, particularly television, have a brief and pyrotechnical ride on the publicity roundabout and are then cast aside and forgotten for ever. Hannah's staying power has proved unique, and now seems unending. Four years after she and her extraordinary lifestyle first came to the public's attention, the Establishment — there is no other word for it — began to seriously consider this phenomenon from a half abandoned Pennine Dale. It was decided that she should be a guest of honour at the Women of the Year Lunch in the Savoy Hotel.

Hannah placed the engraved invitation on her kitchen mantelpiece and prepared to forget about it. She had never been to the capital city and could see no way to go about organising such a momentous trip. The act of trying to find help or sponsorship to bring it about was totally alien to her. Fortunately, one of her constant visitors found out about the invitation and informed Yorkshire Television. And Hannah was persuaded to accept it.

Probably never before have there been two networked television documentaries about the same, apparently ordinary, person. But there she was again, entrancing everyone who came into her company. 'Hannah Goes To Town', a film made by the same team which brought 'Too Long A Winter' to the screen, simply observed Hannah on this trip of a lifetime. Fittingly, the programme was one of the 'Once in a Lifetime' series.

The 'Women of the Year' lunch is an enormously sophisticated affair attended by the most celebrated ladies in the land, all seeking the attention of the reporters and cameramen. Hannah walked into this media mad house, set amid the overwhelming pomp of the Savoy Hotel, wearing a new, if conservative, dress and sensible shoes. Within seconds the cameras and notebooks had deserted the more elegantly draped and coffured guests of honour, most of them household names, and scrambled, shoved and shouted for the attention of a softly spoken Dales farmer.

Hannah did not bat an eyelid, smiled serenely at the cameras and fielded all the questions as only she can. The Household Names stared in blank astonishment. Hannah was unquestionably the Belle of the Ball, and even made the front page splash of one newspaper. A queue of eminent people formed to meet her. One was Lady Mary Wilson, then resident of No. 10, who asked anxiously if all this publicity had spoiled her life. 'Not at all', said Hannah. 'Improved it in fact'.

The Royal Personage on Duty at this upper-class bunfight, the Duchess of Gloucester, asked that Hannah should be added to the privileged line of guests waiting to greet her officially. She proved to be the least overcome of them all. 'You come from the Continent, don't you', inquired Hannah of this friendly Danish lady, who was clearly delighted at such an ingenuous question.

But the one person Hannah desperately wished to meet on this memorable day was not royal, or celebrated in political or business life. She stayed in the background all the time and Hannah despaired of ever exchanging a word with one of the people she admires most of all — Odette Churchill, the war heroine. Towards the end of the affair, word reached Odette who, it turned out, had seen 'Too Long A Winter' and was very keen to meet Hannah. So two shy and somewhat similar people were brought together for a quietly animated discussion. As they parted, Hannah's lips brushed Odette's cheek. It was quite a moment, or, to quote Hannah, 'a

Hannah reading her "fan mail" in the full glare of modern illumination.

dream come true'.

Hannah stayed in a sumptuous riverside suite at the Savoy Hotel ('but I could not sleep — it was too hot') and made a host of new admirers before she returned to the fell in Baldersdale to collect her wellingtons stored in a milk churn and trudge contentedly back to Low Birk Hatt. The resultant documentary was another enormous success and reinforced her position, if that was possible, in the public's estimation.

There was to be yet another, well publicised visit to London when Hannah was invited to Buckingham Palace in 1980 to celebrate the 80th birthday of the Queen Mother. Hannah spent a long time choosing a new floppy hat for that occasion and was pursued down the Mall by a clutch of cameramen. A fresh breeze sprang up outside the Palace and next day newspapers carried sequences of pictures showing Hannah struggling with her headgear. When they left her alone for a few moments and she tried to merge with the crowd to peer at the red-tuniced guards marching around the Palace yard she was recognised and approached by people who had come in hope of a glimpse of quite a different lady. Then she went through the Palace to the lawns and Marquees behind and waited in the line as the Queen Mother and the rest of the Royal family came to greet their guests. 'The most exciting day of my life', she confided afterwards.

Many more, if lesser incidents have crowded into Hannah's life in the decade following that first showing of 'Too Long A Winter'. She receives regular invitations to open fetes, attend various functions, and her name on the posters advertising any event can normally be expected to add a thousand on to the 'gate'. Once, when signing copies of this book, the traffic on the road outside the bookshop was stopped by excited crowds and police had to be called to sort out the chaos. Middle class ladies were heard to exclaim 'I've touched her, I've touched her' as they emerged from a highly successful signing session.

Amidst all this excitement and adulation, the unchanging element in the story of Hannah Hauxwell is Hannah herself. It seems that nothing can affect her. Her character, her outlook, and that unfathomable tranquility has not changed one whit. Women of the Year luncheons, photographs, autograph-hunting fans, even invitations to Buckingham Palace are all peripheral to her life. That will always pivot exclusively on caring for Low Birk Hatt, the farm her family has occupied since it was built, and the animals it houses and which she dotes on. She can afford to keep a dog now, a wayward animal variously called 'Chip' and 'Uffa' which, although a much loved companion, appears to give no practical help at all. But the lonely burden she carries never eases. Indeed, it has increased as a direct result of the material benefits that accrued to her from media exposure. Some of the money which flowed in (and still comes) was spent on more livestock. Instead of having just one cow and one calf to care for, she now has a small herd. It's unlikely that Hannah will ever go hungry again — indeed, certain — but the extra work she has to do, without help of any kind, has grown alarmingly at a time when she should really be looking towards retirement.

Physically, she is growing frailer, an inevitable consequence of the hardships she has endured for so long. Whenever there is a severe winter her 'inner circle' of devoted friends tremble for Hannah. They know she will be toiling through the snowdrifts, dragging a sledge laden with feed for the animals, her breath rasping with the effort and the dull ache of rheumatism in her legs. In the winter of 1978/9 the snow obliterated the dry stone walls and a fierce gale blew down her electricity lines. She had no heat of any kind for four days since her chimney was blocked. The stream which provides her only source of water froze. So did her kettle, and even her false teeth by her bedside. The milk straight from her cow, Rosie, was her only warm drink.

Hannah put three coats on in an attempt to keep out the weather as she struggled through the blizzard to put down feed for her cattle. Each layer of cloth froze solid. 'I looked like a crinoline lady' said a smiling Hannah, demonstrating once again that indomitable spirit which allows no room for self pity.

She is nearing sixty now, and those close enough to her to dare to discuss such a momentous proposition have urgently proposed that she should consider leaving Low Birk Hatt and find a cottage in the comparative comfort and safety of a nearby community. Romaldkirk, where her mother is buried, or, perhaps, the lovely village of Cotherstone. She admits, with much caution, to being tempted by the idea. She agrees that one winter she may collapse and not be found for days, a recurring nightmare which haunts those who hold her dear every time the winter skies thicken with snow.

Postscript

IN the end, she did leave . . . . .

But she held out until the winter of 1988/89, when she was well into pensionable age. Her constant friends had virtually abandoned hope of ever persuading her to vacate Low Birk Hatt and all the perils associated with that unforgiving place.

The move was not without its crises. One was solved when her precious herd of animals found a good home in Baldersdale itself, but uprooting from the place she will always hold dear, the repository of all her treasured memories, was clearly a painful experience for Hannah.

Her land and buildings were sold by tender and the public sale of a few pieces of furniture and farm effects provided a good excuse for her public and the press to turn up and gaze at this singular Dales personality.

The cameras, the interviews, the television news crews . . . once again Hannah took it all serenely in her stride. The column inches and screen time confirmed her enduring status as a media star.

And her name will live on in Baldersdale. Around twenty of her acres were eagerly bought by the Durham Wildlife Trust because they were so rich in wild flowers and a variety of rare grasses as to be virtually unique in the area.

This came about as a direct result of Hannah's farming methods, which allowed nature to nourish her land, not chemical and other inorganic materials. The land will now remain as it always was — unchanged, perhaps, since the Vikings colonised the valley. The Trust's appeal for funds to preserve it drew an international response, including a substantial donation from the Worldwide Fund for Nature.

And this sanctuary will be named after its unwitting founder, Hannah Hauxwell.

Together with the money raised from the remainder of her freehold property, Hannah was able to buy a pleasant, airy cottage in the centre of Cotherstone, which stands prettily at one of the entrances to Baldersdale.

A typically warm and generous Dales welcome awaited her from the locals and the move appears to have been a success. It may take her some time to settle, but in the meantime she relishes water on tap, and central heating, takes tea with other retired ladies and attends Sunday services.

But the major consideration is the security which a community like Cotherstone offers to a maiden lady of uncertain health.

Her fame will assuredly continue well into old age. Yet another major network documentary was being completed by Yorkshire Television as Hannah spent her first summer in Cotherstone. It records the move from Low Birk Hatt and will doubtless stretch the emotions of her countless admirers once again.

There is only one Hannah Hauxwell.

The Dale that Died

A Hidden Place

GEOGRAPHICALLY, Grisedale teeters on the far edge of Upper Wensleydale. But it is a hidden place, an island in a heaving sea of heather and peat protected from common gaze by the possessive embrace of three spectacular fells in the wildest Pennine range.

A million eager tourists pass close by its entrance every summer, hugging road maps that do not even acknowldge the existence of Grisedale, as though the gods which protect its privacy blinded the cartographers when they came to draw this area. Yet Grisedale is, perhaps, the most romantic dale in all Yorkshire, the dream dale which those million people seek, complete in its unspoiled beauty, serenity and vivid history. But no one stumbles across Grisedale. There is only one way into it, for this dale is an enclosed place sealed off at its northern extremity by the impassable heights of Wild Boar Fell. And even this narrow road joins the conspiracy to keep Grisedale a secret. It loops surreptitiously off the main Hawes to Sedbergh highway and will lead the unwary straight back to the main road again. But half way along it is joined by a thin strip of tarmacadam which is unmarked, save for a 'No Through Road' sign. It could be a well-metalled farm track; it is, in fact, the entrance to Grisedale.

This road climbs steeply up the fellside, bisecting rough peat moor, but Grisedale keeps itself hidden for another quarter of a mile. There is a sense of crossing a frontier, heightened by the need to open a gate across the road. At this point, quite suddenly, Grisedale reveals itself, like an Impressionist painting spread before one's feet. On each side the fells soar to more than two thousand two hundred feet and the dale seems to stretch for ever because its conclusion cannot be seen. But it is barely two miles long and half a mile wide.

A deep valley, it veers left in dramatic fashion with the high fells reflecting varying shades of bronze and purple. A beck wanders sinuously through the bottom pastures, fed by streams tumbling amid the familiar pattern of divisive dry-stone walls. On the lower slopes hangs a necklace of farmsteads, mostly in ruins, shedding roof slates and sepia stones in haphazard patterns around their feet.

At first glance Grisedale is a beautiful desolation, echoing in its emptiness. Once, sixteen families in sixteen farms rent the silence with the continuous sounds of living. Now the only persistent voice heard in this valley is the Pennine wind, ruffling the rushes and wild flowers. The loneliness stings the eyes: deserted pastures, gates that are never opened, paths that are never trod. Grisedale is the dale that died. And yet . . . it lives on in the same way that Arthur Pendragon, who once perhaps rode these hills at the head of his cavalry, survives in legend, King of all Kings of England. Grisedale may appear to be extinct but its heart still beats steadily; and it can speak of layer upon layer of life, each boiling with energy, drama, character and every kind of human endeavour. From the dawn of its history until the present day, Grisedale has conducted its affairs in an original and captivating style.

It has always been a special dale, partly a place to hide but mainly a place to live a life without

Grisedale — a hidden place teetering on the far edge of Upper Wensleydale.

interference from the rest of the world. Nineteen hundred years ago, when the warrior chief of the Brigantes, Venutius, broke with his ruler (and wife), Queen Cartimandua, in disgust at her passive capitulation to the Romans, it was to these western dales that he fled to set up resistance. For two decades he raided down towards the east, harassing Brigantian traitors and Romans alike. Centurions built shrines to Silvanus, the god of the wild lands, before setting out to hunt Venutius down, obviously reasoning that they needed all the help they could get in these strange and savage hills. One shrine still survives on the bleak wastes of Scargill Moor, north-east of Grisedale. The Romans eventually destroyed the power of Venutius and enslaved many of his followers in the lead mines of Swaledale (which were still worked well into this century), but others escaped into the remoter dales. Be sure that Grisedale was one of them.

Later inhabitants of the wild region that was Brigantia claimed that from the loins of one of the Dalesman chiefs had sprung, in the fifth century, the most inspirational leader and warrior ever to grace the legends of this land. Now the Arthurian romance is an immensely 'moveable feast', yet in Mallerstang, just a sheep stray over the eastern fell out of Grisedale, there is an ancient castle, now being restored. Among all the Roman, Norse and Danish names in the Yorkshire Dales, contrasting starkly with the thwaites and thorpes, kirkbys and cams, tons and gills, it stands alone: it is called Pendragon Castle.

These local patriots insisted that Arthur was the son of Uther Pendragon of Pendragon Castle, and that he had come frequently to help the men of the dales when they were attacked by the Saxon invaders fighting their way into the Pennines from the east coast. There is support for this claim in the *Historia Britanorum* which refers to an Arthur who fought against the Saxons, riding at the head of a mounted army to wherever his sword was most needed. One of the many glittering threads in the varying tales suggests that Uther Pendragon, accompanied by his principal adviser, Merlin moved to the south-west from Mallerstang. Perhaps Arthur was drawn back in his youth to the land of his fathers or dispatched there to earn his fighting spurs. The records say he specialized in sudden attacks from cover, thundering down upon the Saxons as they beseiged settlements and putting them to rout. Such exploits made him very popular, the super-hero of folklore passed down from generation to generation. There is a story, once widely repeated, that Arthur returned to Yorkshire at the end of his days. He and his Knights are said to be even now sleeping in a cave deep in the rock which supports Richmond Castle, awaiting the call to come to the nation's rescue.

The name of Pendragon Castle marks their association with this land, and the spurs of Arthur may have raked the peat of Grisedale, but a more permanent memorial was left there by those other giants of legend, the Vikings. They established their influence in the area around the tenth century, led by a remarkable figure who rejoiced in the name of Eric Bloodaxe. And they loved places like Grisedale: to this day it remains essentially a Norse hill settlement.

They even gave the dale its name. The word *gris* means pig in the Norse language, and Grisedale is still called the Pig Valley among other Dalesmen. This name has more romantic associations than would first appear. Wild boars ran across Yorkshire's fells and forests in large numbers and were hunted by Brigantes, Romans, Saxons, Danes and Vikings alike. One Roman cavalry leader went so far as to build an altar to Silvanus after killing 'a lovely boar which previous hunters had hunted in vain', while in a later century over on the moors near Whitby a hermit who gave sanctuary to a wild boar in the heat of the chase was put to death by the pursuing noblemen for his impertinence. This unceasing ferocity finally cleared the land of the wild boar but there is a firm tradition in Wensleydale which says that the last surviving pack sought refuge in Grisedale. The looming barrier that seals the north end of the dale bears witness to this claim: Wild Boar Fell.

When the tides of war finally receded and the Pennine dwellers could place self defence lower down the list of priorities the Norsemen made Grisedale into a permanent settlement. The pattern of life they laid down then remains largely undisturbed. They built their long houses with shelter for all — humans and cattle — under one continuous roof. There was one door for the home and another for the byre. The land nearest the houses, nourished by the gentle beck which in winter regularly spills over the banks, became the pasture land for the cattle and swine. The fells supported the sheep. How many times these buildings have been reconstructed can only be guessed at (probably not many) but the foundations in modern Grisedale may well be original.

Their names certainly have the resonance of deep-rooted history: Blake Mire, Round Ing,

High Flust, High Ing, Reacher, Moor Rigg, High Lathe, Fea Foe, Mouse Syke, Clough and Scale. Over the centuries they sheltered unnumbered generations, but now most of them are memorials to the unrecorded people who filled them with hope and despair, laughter and sweat. It is possible to reach back to the early nineteenth century via the keen memories of old Grisedale folk who recall in detail what their grandparents told them. Personal histories before that time stay a secret known only to the implacable fells, but it is likely that the reality outstrips the gaudiest imagination. Nature made Grisedale a setting for drama, a place of extremes, and no inhabitant could have failed to respond.

At the beginning of the last century, sixteen dwellings were occupied, although nothing remains of two or three but a faint scar on the fellside. Grisedale had its own Dame School and the better-off families paid twopence per head per week to have their children taught to read and write. Some, of course, could not afford it: ten or eleven children per household were commonplace.

The basic way of life in Grisedale, however, has scarcely changed for a millennium. It has always been a constant struggle against the harsh environment and even harsher elements. The land is poor and no arable crops can be grown. So powerful are the forces of nature there, it is easy to understand that the inhabitants sought desperately for comfort and guidance. They turned avidly to religion.

Because of their fierce individualism it was natural that they should reject the established religious order for something more personal and elemental. Grisedale has never conformed so when the teachings of George Fox filtered through to the Dales they received an eager response there and throughout Wensleydale.

Several farms were used for gatherings until proper Meeting Houses could be built. Fox's chief disciple was Richard Robinson of Countersett Hall in Raydale, where the founder himself spent a night in 1677. Grisedale embraced Quakerism and with it all the inevitable trouble which accompanies revolutionary thought. These curious people and their silent services disturbed the local Establishment and they were relentlessly persecuted, particularly by the Metcalfes of Nappa Hall who once ruled Wensleydale like monarchs. The reluctance of the Quakers to pay tithes (mainly wool, cheese and hand-knitted goods) led to their possessions being seized and they could be fined large amounts just for holding their meetings. In Grisedale the Quakers wisely conducted their affairs near to Scale Farm, which is as far as buildings go on the west side. There is still evidence of one of their burial grounds on the Scale pastures.

But Grisedale reserved its real religious fervours for another new ideal—the concept of Methodism as preached by John Wesley. He held a meeting in Hawes, the principal market town of Upper Wensleydale, and the manner of his coming is still talked about. The story goes that Wesley travelled from Barnard Castle to preach on a hillside at Low Row in Swaledale, where there was a long established Congregational Chapel. Hearing afterwards that there was another, more populous, place called Wensleydale just over the fells, he declared his intention of walking over there immediately. But he was told that the way was too dangerous for a stranger and he would get lost on the wild and pot-holed Buttertubs moorland. Wesley so badly wanted to go that the Low Row Congregationalists finally lent him a horse. It is still known for Wensleydale Congregationalists to conclude an argument with Methodists with: 'Well, John Wesley wouldn't have come to Wensleydale if he hadn't been lent a Congregational horse, and you lot would still be heathens!'

The word of Wesley spread like a bracken fire across the moors, engulfing Grisedale and all the communities along Wensleydale to Sedbergh. There is no record of Wesley penetrating in

Grisedale — a beautiful desolation, echoing in its emptiness.

person further than Hawes but the message he preached became the pivot of life for the best part of a century in Grisedale. For the dale found its own religious leader, an evangelist of such extraordinary powers that his influence and personality are still tangible.

He was called Richard Atkinson.

Inspired and encouraged by him, the heads of several households studied the art of public speaking to become lay preachers. One followed the other into the highly varnished pulpits of the tiny chapels being built by the converts throughout the valleys each delivering his own particular brand of fire and brimstone. Fiddle playing was condemned, dancing was called the invention of the Devil, card-playing was even worse and as for drink . . . well, they reserved their fiercest rhetoric for all forms of alcoholic liquor. Astonishingly, illicit sex was not on the hellfire and damnation list in Grisedale. Elsewhere it was the worst sin of all, but in Grisedale it seems that a general amnesty was declared in that purple zone on the wrong side of the blanket.

Twice every Sunday a solemn procession would wend its way down the winding, rock-strewn track along Grisedale and out to the nearest chapel. Men in their best fustians and fob watches, women in their black hats and neck-to-ankle dresses, children in prickly Sabbath clothes. On special occasions such as anniversaries it would occur three times, for morning, afternoon and evening services.

Only the memory of those pious times remains. Like a loving old couple, Grisedale and Methodism declined slowly together, hand in hand. Both are still alive and still fighting the old enemies but the vigour has diminished, the passion diffused into sad tolerance and the tiny chapels made large by their dwindling congregations. The Methodists are still the principal guardians of religion in Upper Wensleydale and their presence can be felt in practical terms. There is, for instance, only one public house along the entire fifteen miles between Hawes and Sedbergh, a road which passes through the completely dry village of Garsdale at the mouth of Grisedale. A handful of old men and women, with faith undimmed, keep the chapels open but their evangelism is worn thin by public indifference.

There has been no successor to Richard Atkinson.

In 1969 the very spirit of Grisedale faltered and nearly died. Just one dwelling was still occupied and run as a farm and the occupants gave notice to quit. But into the dale came a remarkable man to nourish the continuity of its life, to keep the centuries of Grisedale's history invested with real meaning.

Joe Gibson is smaller in stature than the average Grisedalian and was only five years away from the accepted retirement age when he came. Joe and his wife were not even remotely born to these hills, and knew nothing about how to live with them. But Joe possesses one ancient local quality — an aggressive ability to overcome disadvantages, born of long years of struggle which began in a place he calls the nearest to hell on earth. He also happened to be a Methodist lay preacher of thirty years' experience. It was as though the ghosts of Grisedale past had selected him for the task.

In between Richard Atkinson and Joe Gibson the story of Grisedale, a place considered too insignificant to be noticed, is a complete pageant of everything people hold dear about the Yorkshire Dales.

The Legend of Richard Atkinson

SOMEWHERE close to the mellow sandstone walls of Grouse Hall, which lies a few yards, away from the entrance to Grisedale, a thorn tree once flourished, notable for the two matching holes in the ground beneath it. They were quarried by the knees of Richard Atkinson as he prayed mightily each day at dawn for the remission of the sins of Grisedale.

Richard Atkinson was a gamekeeper of unprepossessing appearance who died prematurely at the age of forty almost one hundred years ago. Yet he remains a burning legend throughout the western dales, and the mention of his name will bring an instant response from older Dalesfolk. He may be the most remembered man ever to come out of Wensleydale; certainly he was the most remarkable. More even than John Wesley, he was the spiritual father of a wide area. And he gave his heart to Grisedale.

Richard Atkinson did not always cut such a pious figure. According to Christopher Pratt, eminent Grisedalian, a leading authority on Atkinson's life and times and a man who helps to carry on his tradition in the pulpit, Richard was 'a Godless, pleasure-loving young man.' He was a spirited fiddleplayer much in demand at dances and parties and an enthusiastic card player. He even mocked the religious and it seems likely that he also flirted with the Demon Drink. On the local Wesleyan roll of the damned, the name of young Richard Atkinson was prominent.

The details of his conversion are not recorded, but it came shortly after a most outrageous incident. Apparently Dick and some of his raucous companions were passing a Dales chapel as a service was in progress and he was dared to dance up to the front aisle and back out again. Dick promptly accepted the challenge, but as he capered among the astonished congregation one of his leggings inexplicably flew off. This strange incident worried Dick enormously. He began to see it as an omen of impending disaster in payment for his act of folly, a sign from Heaven. Shortly afterwards he offered himself for conversion.

Chris Pratt, now in his seventies, remembers from his youth how the old people still talked of the conversion of Dick Atkinson: 'It was the wonder of the Dales, there being few more Godless or greater sinners. But he became most zealous in God's service. My great-grandfather, Jim Brunskill of High Hall in Lunds, said he never knew anyone with such mighty faith as Dick Atkinson.'

The new convert then developed a strange power. He began to see the future and there are many stories of his ability and willingness publicly to predict events.

Curiously, however, little is known about the early past of Richard Atkinson and, what is more inexplicable for such a famous person, no well documented description of his physical appearance exists. Chris Pratt asked several of the children (all dead themselves now) of people who knew him well and the only definite information came from one who said he looked very much like the late Matthew Bell, who lived on Raydaleside. Matthew was believed to be a great-nephew of Dick Atkinson, and he was a spare, pale man of below medium height with great energy — and a squint. Until recently, it was thought that no photograph of Dick Atkinson

existed although he was a public figure during the start of the great Victorian craze for photography. His direct descendants do not possess one, nor do they ever recall any family reference to a photograph of Dick. There are several photographs of his wife, but the theory is that Dick avoided cameras because of his squint. During the autumn of 1974, however, one tiny print was found in a collection owned by a distant relative who said that her grandmother stoutly maintained that it was a photograph of Dick Atkinson. The person in the fading sepia is dressed as a gamekeeper, with gun in hand and a Yorkshire terrier at his feet. Measured against the chair in which he is sitting he seems below medium height, and he is certainly a spare figure, with tight lips and a determined jaw. And through the mist which obscures the fine detail of his face, his eyes appear to glide towards each other.

Information about Dick's childhood is equally scant, but it seems clear he was raised in Pendragon country around Mallerstang. He came from a large family which apparently shared the mystic quality Dick used to such effect after his conversion. Chris Pratt talked once to a lady who many years ago worked for a Mrs. Blyth in Hawes, who was Dick's sister, and remembered her employer recalling that her father had the gift of foresight. But his power was limited to forecasting death whereas his son's went beyond this gloomy area. Apparently the unhappy ability which Dick's father possessed has been passed on to his descendants. Chris Pratt knows one who wishes it had not.

'She's called Hattie Mackie and she lives in Earby. She's a descendant of one of Dick's sisters and comes to see a cousin in this area. I've talked to her a few times and she tells me that on two or three occasions whilst visiting relations she has realized they were going to die. She says its an awful feeling.'

Dick Atkinson was numbered among that exclusive band of Dalesmen who never had to worry about a livelihood because of their amazing skill with animals. Long before the advent of veterinary surgeons (and long after) they went around curing sheep with the sturdy, cows that wouldn't yield and lame horses, for grateful farmers. They used herbs, flowers and berries collected from the hedgerows and moors and made their own potions, ointments and pills. Once again, it was often a skill passed down from father to son.

Dick became quite a celebrated figure as he toured the dales to treat animals before he was hired as a gamekeeper by a Mr. Batty and came to live at Grouse Hall. After his conversion he ceremoniously placed his fiddle and playing cards on the fire and threw himself into spreading the message of Wesley around the dales. He had a tolerant employer in Mr. Batty who, though 'a heavy drinker and man of the world', admired the principles of his gamekeeper. On one occasion Dick was beating for one of Mr. Batty's shooting parties when a guest offered him a drink. Dick, naturally, refused. This annoyed the guest to such an extent that he reported the insolence to Mr. Batty, remarking that he would sack any of his employees who refused to drink with him.

'And I', said Mr. Batty 'would give all I possess to be as good a man as Dick.'

In later years when Mr. Batty lay dying, he sent for Dick and asked him to pray with him. This he did with his usual vigour, but afterwards Mr. Batty said: 'It's no use Dick. All's as black as night. I've sinned away my day of grace.'

Opposite: **Believed to be the only photograph of Richard Atkinson, dressed as a game-keeper with his Yorkshire terrier at his feet.**

Dick's energy, and prodigious strength when he required it, helped him when he came up against an employer not so generous as Mr. Batty. This man owned a farm in Wensleydale and hired Dick to help at haytime. Whenever the weather was too damp to mow Dick would start preaching to whoever among his fellow labourers would listen and then try to gather support for evening services. This angered his boss, who worked out a plan to stop Dick. He instructed his son, renowned for his size and strength, to wield his scythe at such a speed that Dick would be too exhausted trying to keep pace with him to hold his services after sunset.

The contest began, and the tall grass fell at a rate never seen before in Wensleydale; the sun reflected off the whistling scythes on to the sweat glistening on their arms and faces. It ended when the son became ill with the strain and capitulated. Before the end of that momentous haytime he fell under the spell of Dick and was converted. The following winter Dick was asked to hold evangelical services in the same area and among those who came forward were the boss and his wife. Dick's triumph was complete.

Stories like this circulated round the dales and when Dick climbed into the pulpit on Sundays he began to face crowded pews. He responded in characteristic fashion, regularly preaching up a storm of good humoured faith and occasionally galvanising his listeners with remarkable outbursts. After one enormously successful revival service he had persuaded every member of the congregation to come forward and re-dedicate his life to the Lord, and as they knelt before him weeping and shouting 'Hallelujah' he is said to have leant forward and suddenly declared: 'I've a good mind to go away home, get my gun and shoot the lot of you.' During the shocked silence which followed, one person plaintively asked: 'Why, Dick, why?' And he replied: 'Because when you leave this Chapel tonight I know you'll go back to your sinful ways but if I shoot you all now you'll be saved!'

But that incident was a minor affair compared with one utterance he made from the pulpit, which became one of Wensleydale's favourite legends. He was delivering one of his absorbing sermons to an attentive audience which included a young girl he had never seen before. Without any warning he stopped preaching, stared at the girl and pointed. 'You are to be my wife,' he announced. The wide eyes of the congregation moved from one to the other. 'The Lord's just told me you are to be my wife,' he confirmed, and then calmly went on with his sermon.

This story may have been slightly dramatized down the years but there is firm evidence that Dick did see his wife for the first time at a revival meeting, and before they had been introduced announced to his friends that he was going to marry her. What is absolutely certain is that Mary Moore was Heaven-sent. Apart from being generally accepted as 'the bonniest lass in Clapham,' a flying start to any arranged romance, she was accustomed to the sort of hard and lonely life she would inevitably lead as the mate of a roving evangelist. She was the daughter of a 'scholarly and God-fearing' farmer but she had two uncles who spent everything they had on drink. When she was twelve her mother died and she had to run the home, care for her brother and sisters and cope with her drunken, impoverished uncles. Their marriage was worthy of a lengthy account in *Finny's Journal,* a leading local newspaper, dated June 1872.

Tragedy also touched Dick's life before he was married and he predicted that it would happen. He lived with his grandmother and a sister at Grouse Hall and after finishing work on the fells.

Opposite: **Chapel in the dale — Hawes Junction.**

regularly made for preaching engagements all round Wensleydale. Always a man in a hurry, he habitually ignored the roads and struck out directly over the fells to save time. Now fells around Grisedale are delightful places for hiking by day when the paths and tracks are sunlit and well defined, but they become deadly places by night when the mists swirl down, and even the men reared to these moors could—and sometimes did—stumble into the black peat bogs which digest the unwary with one slimey swallow. Dick had criss-crossed the fells without incident a hundred times (thereby enhancing his reputation). But one night as he returned through the mists from a stint in a Dent chapel he said he saw a vision of his grandmother enveloped in flames (peat bog gas does occasionally ignite). Before he set out the following night to preach again he instructed his sister not to leave their grandmother. During his sermon, he is said to have stopped in mid sentence, and then declared that he must go home becuase he was sure something had happened to his grandmother. And when he returned she was dead. His sister had gone into the field outside to bring in some washing and during her absence their grandmother fell on to the fire.

Another of his visions was just as macabre. It happened when he was preaching in Grisedale, which did not have its own chapel in those days; the Methodists borrowed the meeting house from the kindly Quakers (who refused to sell it to their overwhelming rivals in faith). As he spoke, Dick saw a coffin bearing the name of a well known woman in Grisedale and sadly informed his friends that she was to die. Soon after, on 24th March 1882, the woman gave birth to a daughter and fell seriously ill. Dick attended her deathbed and declared he could see four angels, one at each corner of the bed, who melted away when she finally died. Her child survived to bear two sons and four daughters of her own but she also died prematurely, in her forties.

Dick's supernatural powers were not easily accepted in Grisedale and he became resigned to occasionally submitting to a test. One of his earliest challenges came on Baugh Fell, when he encountered three or four sceptical Grisedalians who had gone there to gather sheep. But a mist had suddenly shrouded the higher slopes and hidden the sheep. One of the frustrated men turned to Dick and said in a bantering way: 'Dost'a think it would clear if thou prayed, Dick?' Said Dick: 'Dost'a think it wouldn't clear if I did?'

With that Dick fell to his knees and prayed. The mist cleared.

Dick's knees had to absorb an amazing amount of wear over the years following his conversion because he believed firmly in the power of prayer. According to his grand-daughters, his wife, Mary, attributed his success as an evangelist and his gift of second sight to constant prayer. Sometimes he would pray all through the night if he was concerned about a particular church or individual, and the two knee holes under the thorn tree got deeper by the year, even though corduroy of the time could not take this sort of punishment and his trousers were regularly in a sad state. Once he met his friend and fellow preacher, Joseph Henry Wilson of Garsdale, on a visit to Hawes, who insisted on taking him to a tailor.

'Measure Dick for a pair of breeches,' he declared. 'He's worn his out at the knees praying to keep you fellows out of Hell.'

Dick's wife also told her grand-daughters that he knew in advance what would happen at his services and that he must not conclude them until it came to pass. The great achievement of an evangelist is, of course, to secure conversions and it is said that Dick always knew how many there would be and sometimes would identify the converts — by name if they were local people, or by description of dress, sex and age if strangers to the dale. Evangelistic services in the old days — and occasionally even now — bore no relation to the quiet, devout occasions laced with a few quavering hymns which are standard today in most churches, Anglican or Noncomformist. They were rumbustious, exciting affairs with people leaping to their feet to shout 'Hallelujahs' and give passionate testimony to their faith. The conversion of a known sinner would galvanize a congregation. A special bench was always placed before the pulpit to receive converts and the climax to any service came when they rose from their pews, often in floods of tears, to advance down the aisle to kneel at the bench and dedicate their lives to Christ. Some emotional people were 'converted' regularly, unable to resist the hypnotic appeal of a gifted evangelist, but Dick Atkinson genuinely changed the lives of hundreds of people.

In his day, congregations were prepared to stay with an eloquent preacher a good deal longer than they would now but there was one famous occasion when Dick went on so long that even he could not hold them. Three young men had rolled into that service somewhat the worse for drink, listened for a while and then departed noisily. Dick promptly launched the congregation into joint prayers for the conversion of the three and would not stop. After several hours he had exhausted even the most faithful, so he carried on alone. One of his flock did return to bring him food, and the vigil went on until just before midnight, when the chapel door opened and in came the three young men to kneel before the pulpit and ask to be received. Apparently they had spent a long time together standing on a bridge fighting a strange impulse to return and repent.

Dick's weary comment as they made their nervous appearance was: 'Nay lads, why did you keep me waiting so long?'

There was another marathon session during a Sunday visit to Bainbridge. Following the afternoon service he wandered over to the river, which has always been good trout water, and saw five fish. This he took as a sign that there would be five conversions that evening, and sure enough five young men came to the service and sat together in a back pew. But as the main service ended, and before Dick had time to issue his invitation to make the decision and come forward, they rose and left. Promptly, Dick knelt and said 'I'm staying here, Lord, until you bring them back.' They came. It took a deal of hard praying by Dick, but they came. It is believed that one of the five was the late Alexander Kirkbridge, who went on to become a preacher.

Another remarkable incident involved a well known local man called Jim Allen, who died just short of eighty in the 1930s. He was in the congregation for an evening service at Garsdale Street Chapel, a marvellous little place tacked on to a terraced row of houses which still has a permanent bench devoted exclusively to converts (seldom used these days, of course). Dick conducted the service and after Jim, a bearded man of small stature, had filed out with most of the congregation Dick asked some of the chapel members to stay behind. 'I want you to pray with me for Jim Allen,' he explained. 'I know he's gone out but he will return, for he is under the influence of God's Spirit.'

By chance, Jim Allen was only just outside the chapel door when Dick said this and heard every word. He listened for a while and then went to report to his friends. 'Do you know, they are praying for me back there,' he said. 'They think I'm going to get converted tonight but they are mistaken. I shall do nothing of the kind.'

But the strange power of Richard Atkinson began inevitably to work on Jim and he later went back to the chapel and straight to the special bench. His entire family became staunch Methodists — his son began to preach (he died of typhoid fever at the age of thirty-six), and then his grandson. Today Jim Allen's great-grandsons are familiar sights in the pulpits around Grisedale, a striking example of the continuity of Dick's influence.

Triumphs like these spurred Dick on and he spent more and more nights on his knees seeking guidance and fore-knowledge, much to the concern of Mary, who saw his health beginning to suffer. Stories about him began to spread all round the Dales and into the industrial towns and cities, and people travelled long distances to see him. He always seemed to know they were coming. Once he travelled several miles to West Burton to hold revival meetings through the weekend and lodged with an inquisitive old lady. Knowing of Dick's reputation for forecasting, she asked him whether there would be any converts that night. Dick was not too keen on being constantly cross-examined about his unusual ability but the old lady pressed hard, and to gain some peace he eventually told her that there would be just one. Instead of satisfying her, this unleashed a barrage of questions about the identity of the person. Dick again had to concede and said it would be a woman, describing her in detail, right down to the kind of hat and coat she would be wearing. On hearing this, his hostess declared (no doubt with prim triumph) that Dick was surely mistaken this time. 'There is no woman in this locality who fits your description,' she said.

She was wrong, of course. The conversion occurred exactly as Dick had predicted: the woman he described had arrived in the village from Liverpool the day before.

This incident was virtually duplicated at another service arranged at another chapel some distance away from Dick's home. When the time came for Dick to start travelling a storm began to blow. There was no covered transport for Dick and his friends urged him not to go, assuring him that no one would turn up on such a night. But Dick said he had to go for there would be a convert. One again he described a woman completely unknown in the dale, this time pinpointing the place where she would sit. So off he went. Around the same time a train came into Garsdale station and a woman alighted to ask the way to the chapel where Richard Atkinson would be preaching. Apparently, news of his evangelism had reached her and she wanted his help. She disappeared into the storm and walked a considerable distance before her dripping figure appeared at the chapel door for her predestined meeting and conversion.

As the 1880s dawned, Dick's reputation had grown to enormous proportions and even reached London, which was a remarkable feat of communication in the middle nineteenth century when London and the Dales were as separate as the earth and the moon. He was invited to preach in the capital but after much deliberation and the inevitable hours of prayer he decided that his mission should be confined to the Yorkshire Dales.

He gathered around him a group of fellow evangelists who became known throughout the western dales as Dick Atkinson's Disciples. They went out on their own and in groups to start up missions in the towns and villages surrounding Grisedale. Another well known Atkinson legend tells the story of how two of his team tried to launch a mission in Hawes, the same Joseph Henry Wilson who bought Dick a new pair of breeches and Richard Harper from Pot Gill. They tried hard, but found Hawes a cold place full of sceptics and there were no conversions at all. Eventually, they gave in and miserably began the journey back home. One version of this story has Dick asleep at home during the pair's retreat. He is said to have woken up suddenly, declaring that the Devil was at work close by and he must go to challenge him. Another has Dick on the moors above Grisedale carrying out his duties as gamekeeper (evangelism was always a labour of love for him) when he had a vision of the two men being pursued from Hawes by the Devil. Whichever way he got to know, he certainly hurried down to intercept his friends and tell them that 'we cannot allow the Devil to drive men from God's work' and urge them to return. He dispelled their reluctance with the assurance that if they returned and tried once more they would succeed magnificently.

A Richard Atkinson prediction of that kind was, by now, irresistible and the pair obeyed. That night the greatest revival ever known in Hawes began, and the chapel was said to be crowded with penitents. One conversion followed another in quick succession and Hawes

The market place at Sedbergh. A very early photograph, probably over a century old.

became a Methodist stronghold from then on.

The Devil was very real to Dick and he reported several personal encounters to his close friends. Once when he was cutting peat on the moors the Devil appeared to be in the next peat pot, mocking Dick and his efforts to spread his faith. Dick responded in typical fashion — he knelt to pray and the daunting vision slowly disappeared. For several years before he died, Dick grew a beard because he said he felt that the Devil was holding his hand and trying to make him cut his throat with the razor when he shaved.

Perhaps the last major mission Dick ever undertook was also his greatest. It happened at Sedbergh, which had not had a revival for many years and the elders of the chapel were worried at the lack of support in the town. They went, as so many did, to Grouse Hall to ask Dick's advice and he is supposed to have said: 'Give me three days, and then I'll tell you what God says.' He then went to look down upon the old market town, which marks the place where the two great northern regions of beauty, the Dales and the Lakes, reach over to each other. He saw a mist coming out of the Public Hall, spreading round the town and penetrating up an adjoining dale. When the elders came back he told them to hire the Public Hall, nominated another evangelist to lead the onslaught and promised to help personally. They did as he said but laboured for a week with no return — and what's more, Dick did not turn up for a single meeting. When he did finally present himself after walking the eight miles from Grouse Hall they turned on him angrily and declared: 'You don't appear to be much concerned about the sinners of Sedbergh.' What they did not know (and apparently he did not tell them) was that he had spent the week in prayer, again without much sleep.

But he turned their rebukes into mute apology by climbing into the pulpit and weaving the Atkinson spell once again. The Sedbergh mission went on for sixteen consecutive and tumultuous weeks and went down in local history as 'The Great Revival'. The previous gloom in the Public Hall was transformed as the sinners came surging forward to ask for acceptance, sometimes eight at a time. It is believed that for a long time most Methodist local preachers working the Sedbergh circuit had been converted in that mission. And several of the men who struggle to keep Methodism alive today had their fire kindled by the Atkinson spark, once removed. Chris Pratt is a typical case: 'I was converted on July 4th, 1915, at a meeting in Grisedale. The preacher who received me was Dick Harper, the auctioneer, who was one of Dick Atkinson's converts in the Sedbergh revival.'

The tremendous physical strain of Sedbergh and countless hundreds of other feats of evangelism inevitably damaged Dick's health. Constant travelling on foot and horse in the ferocious Dales winters and years of forsaking sleep for prayer whilst doggedly working on as a gamekeeper during the daylight hours finally forced him to take to his bed. Consumption was diagnosed. Dick fought back with prayer and is said to have visited a Faith Healer. He did rally for a time after this but relapsed shortly afterwards and it is believed that the last time he came downstairs was on the funeral day of one of his daughters. He died himself at 7.15 a.m. on 31st May, 1884; he was in his forty-first year. By his side was his old friend and fellow evangelist, Richard Harper of Pot Gill, one of the two disciples ordered to return to Hawes.

He said that as Richard Atkinson's life finally ebbed away, the room appeared to be full of angels.

When the news of his death spread, the grief experienced throughout Wensleydale was unprecedented. A deep depression settled on the Methodist cause along the chain of chapels from Hawes to Sedbergh which Dick had dominated with his spiritual strength and example for so long. But the traditional hardiness of Dalesfolk soon burst the bonds of mourning. They are raised to meet despair with optimism and the harsh nature of their lives allows little room for sentiment.

They rationalized Dick's early death in a brutally simple but effective manner, saying that perhaps it was as well that he died when he did because they were in danger of crediting him with such spiritual power that they might have placed more trust in him than in God. Some even said that his influence for good was waning, that his stern modesty was beginning to crumble in the face of such sustained hero worship.

In Grisedale, they met the disaster in a typically practical way. To show ther gratitude for the many gifts he brought them, they set about the ruins of the old abandoned farmsteads and scoured the fellside for other suitable stones. With their bare hands they carried them half a mile down the valley and began to build a tiny chapel, on a site near to the beck, in between Mouse Syke and Moor Rigg. They laboured for five years and the final act before they held the opening service was to place a heavy tablet in the gable-end facing the road. It was inscribed: 'The Richard Atkinson Memorial Wesleyan Chapel.'

Mary Atkinson lived on for nearly fifty years after the death of her husband. She left the dale almost immediately (perhaps she was obliged to, if Grouse Hall went with Richard's employment) and moved to Bentham with her three surviving children, all daughters, raising enough money to live by taking up nursing in private homes. She had lost an only son and two other daughters before her husband died.

Although Mary lived in the mighty shadow cast by her husband and was described as an unobtrusive and somewhat shy person, she also had great strength of character and at least one Atkinson legend belongs to her alone. She enthusiastically shared Dick's belief in the power of prayer and seemingly put it to use on one remarkable occasion during her later life in Bentham.

She had gone to visit relatives in Shipley, near Bradford, and was returning home by train. To her consternation she realized that she had boarded the Heysham boat express by mistake. Now that train was a familiar sound in Bentham as it thundered through every night at eleven o'clock and had never been known to stop. Mary was carrying very little money, knew no one in Heysham and was worried about the inevitable alarm at home if she failed to appear. So she prayed. As the express approached Greystone Ghyll bridge it began to slow down, and finally came to a halt in Bentham station. It had run short of water.

Her amazed fellow passengers, no doubt already intrigued by the old lady's praying watched as she bade them goodnight and stepped on to the platform. Only once, and many years later, was that train known to stop at Bentham station again and that was prearranged for the benefit of a passenger left behind on an excursion.

The evangelical blood of Richard Atkinson has been carried down his line: the third and fourth generations are continuing the work he started. All six of his grandchildren became church members and officers, including Margaret Clapham, who was accepted as a fully accredited local preacher in 1947, and Margaret Mansergh, a well known solo singer in many chapels since her conversion. In 1958, great-grand-daughter Rosemary Barrett married John Beyer when he became a full-time Baptist minster, specializing in evangelism among young people.

Mary Atkinson died in the summer of 1933. Half a century before, when she stood at her husband's graveside in Garsdale one of Dick Atkinson's disciples came to comfort her, saying 'Well, you will meet again in Heaven.' To which she replied: 'Yes, but he will be so near the Throne I may not be able to get near him.'

Haymaking in Upper Wensleydale about fifty years ago.

Decline and Fall

THE last two decades of the nineteenth century proved cataclysmic in the affairs of Grisedale. Indeed, it was a bad time for the whole of Upper Wensleydale and the ordered pattern of life in its quiet valleys was seriously disturbed.

Sixteen families still clung tenaciously to life along the slopes of Grisedale, but some of them only had smallholdings with tiny acreages of pasture land for their cattle. In that other land beyond the hills where the earth is generous and yielding and the climate Mediterranean by comparison, trouble came ten years earlier. Four ruinously wet summers bankrupted agriculture in the south of England and the 1881 census revealed that one hundred thousand men had left the land during the previous decade. Agriculture in the higher dales is far more defensive and wet summers not unusual. In Grisedale the only arable crop is grass for winter feed and if the elements allow a little breathing space to get it cut and dried then all is well. But the general depression and the economic pressures of the industrial revolution finally found and penetrated Grisedale and it became clear that a man could no longer live and raise a family on the income from a few sheep, two or three cows and a sow. The death of Richard Atkinson was the prelude to disaster in Grisedale and it is hardly surprising that it took the men who farmed it five years to complete the chapel in his memory. As they hauled the stone to the site and began to build, the dale began to collapse about them.

One by one, eight farms were abandoned. Eight sorry processions carrying their belongings wended out of the valley and into oblivion. Who most of these people were, their names and achievements, is not within the memory of the descendants of the families which survived. Most likely they were swallowed up by the mills of the West Riding: how they must have hated it, those men descended from ancestors who had responded to the call of the fells for a thousand years.

The remaining families fought on, and other brave souls moved in to take up the challenge when they quit. Christopher Pratt was four when he first came to Grisedale as his father, Bell, took over the tenancy of Round Ing. But the Pratts were no strangers to the valley: Chris's grandmother, who lived in Lunds, had been one of the pupils at the twopence per week Dame School.

Bell Pratt, who was thirty at the time, and his wife, Elizabeth, raised another five children in the dale. Round Ing was one of the smallest and most exposed farms and life was a relentless struggle of trying to make ends meet. Grisedale has poor, wet land with a black, peaty top soil and a stubborn layer of clay underneath. On his share of it Bell could never keep more than twelve cows, including three milkers, and about ninety breeding ewes. His eldest child, Chris, recalls long years of hardship.

'Nobody had any brass to spare in Grisedale but Round Ing was pretty much at the bottom of

Opposite: **Chris Pratt in the 1970s outside his home, Low Moor, in Garsdale.**

52

Lunds School, about 1920.

the league. We had just enough to exist on. Sometimes now I wonder just how we did lead a life, with all those children. We just had to be self supporting. Mother would make butter from the milk and every other Monday William Hodgson Harper who had the shop at Hawes Junction would come into the dale with his horse and covered wagon to barter, stopping at Moor Rigg to set up for business. He would take our eggs and butter to sell at market and we'd get flour, salt, oatmeal and corn for the cattle in return, or money if we were stocked up.

'Making the butter was quite a job. We didn't have a separator so we'd have to skim off the cream by running a finger round the top of the pail and pouring it into a pot. There would be a churning day once a week and we all had to take turns at the handle. We had a peculiar churner. It was square with wooden paddles and it took all our strength to keep them moving because it took a fair quantity of cream. It was mainly a summer job when the cows were milking well and we'd get about ten or twelve pounds of butter to sell at nine or tenpence a pound. In winter the price would go up to more than a shilling but we sometimes only churned one pound.

'We kept twenty hens and the eggs would sell at ten to seventeen a shilling depending on the season, but none were laid for three months during winter because we had no modern methods of feeding. We gave 'em whole India corn, big pieces straight out of the husk, which William Hodgson Harper kept in a considerable warehouse he had over the shop. He used to supply all the feedstuff to the dale because he was an agent in quite a big way, buying and selling all manner of goods.

'We depended on our sheep for a good piece of our living. The wool was clipped every year and then we might get a crop of about eighty-five lambs. Half of them were always kept to replace the old draft ewes which had yielded a third crop and the other half were sold together with the outgoing ewes.

'Our wool used to go to Sharman's of Bradford, but we had to pay for the carting of it to the warehouse at Kirkby Stephen. They'd pay us between threepence and fivepence a pound. Our ninety breeding ewes and the thirty gimmer hogs [first year sheep] would give about 360 lbs.

'We never bought stock if we could help it, only the occasional heifer calf. Bull calves we bred were sold off because we were trying to keep a milk herd. We had one horse, a small dales cob with a bit of Clydesdale in him.

'Like everyone else we kept a pig. And we were so poor that we largely depended on that pig for our food. Breakfast was always porridge and then we children would have sandwiches packed to take for our lunch when we walked over to school in Lunds — it was right on the tops that place and I always claimed to have been to High School. Most times there would be no meat so the sandwiches were spread with bacon fat, which I got to like so well that I still prefer it to butter. When we came home there would always be potatoes in a pan on the boiler top and we'd eat them for dinner with a bit of bacon. It was always our chief meat, fried bacon. We had very little fresh meat. In autumn, Tom Harper at Mouse Syke used to butcher one sheep every week and hawk it round the dale. Sometimes we'd have a bit of mutton off him, and sometimes one of our fat lambs might go lame or get hurt some other way and we'd kill and eat that.

'And we'd always be on the look out for rabbits. To children today a rabbit is something to point at and admire but to us it was a meal — good meat. As soon as we were big enough to catch them we never missed a chance. If we saw one going into a wall three or four of us would go either side and corner it. Or if it went into an old rabbit nest — they were about three foot long — we would dig it out and kill it by striking with our hands. We used to think a rabbit pie was a real treat.

'We had no gun at our farm but sometimes grandfather and Uncle Tom would come over with one from Hell Gill in Mallerstang to shoot us one or two.'

The kind of hunger generated in those healthy young stomachs as they walked and ran for miles each day in the fresh air once spurred them to remarkable lengths. One winter's day a kestrel was hovering at the bottom of the Round Ing pastures in pursuit of game, unaware that several other pairs of keen eyes were watching it. A fat wood pigeon flapped steadily into the sky beneath the deadly claws of the kestrel and the young audience watched tensely as the hunter banked sharply and made an unerringly accurate dive and strike. The wood pigeon crashed into the field and the hawk wheeled to pick up his meal. But rival hunters were already pounding down the pasture as he settled and the astonished kestrel was beaten away.

'Aye, it went into our pot did that pigeon', says Chris. 'We plucked it and we ate it. It was good, too.'

But even this incident pales before the desperation of one Grisedale family. They went down to the beck and threw in a bucketful of lime to stun the fish. Several trout floated to the surface and Chris Pratt maintains that these people ate them uncooked, so acute was their hunger.

Christmas brought the only certain break in the Pratt's spartan diet. However the last year had gone, good or bad, and a big effort was made in the kitchen.

'Aye, it was one time when we knew we would sit down to a tremendous good feed, followed by a plum pudding. It was traditional to pick out a real good cock chicken from one of the two broods we had each year and fatten him specially for Christmas. And we always had a stocking. There was an aunt at Settle who didn't marry until late and she usually sent us a few bits of toys and a spiced sugar pig. And we'd get an apple and an orange. The orange was a big treat because we didn't see many of them.

'But I don't remember my mother and father exchanging presents — I don't think it would run to that.'

There were many diversions for youngsters in Grisedale and during the childhood of Chris the junior population numbered around twenty. Winter always brought superb sledging and the beck was a constant source of fun. One of the favourite pastimes was to play 'farm' on the banks, building enclosures with stones and using fir cones for sheep and white-flecked pebbles for cows. There were cranberries to pick on the fells and all those derelict farms to play in. But the fascinating ruins were carefully avoided after dusk, and some of the more remote ones at all times.

'You see, ghosts were a very prominent thing in Grisedale. Folks used to be terrible for telling bits of ghost tales when I was a lad, like, and they seemed to believe them. There was one old chap who went down to a cow hut near one of the abandoned places and he heard some groaning. He was supposed to do some milking but he vanished rapidly leaving the cow unmilked because he was sure it was a ghost. Probably it would be a sheep. Anyway, tales like that frightened us children so much that we would walk miles to avoid going near some of them ruins. There were just one or two we would play in during daylight.'

Communication between the outside world and Grisedale was kept to a minimum. After all, travel usually incurred unnecessary expense and if you chose to walk it was an awful long way to Hawes. People who came to inspect the kind of life led in the valley were not impressed.

'They reckoned they came from civilized parts,' says Chris. 'They always said something like "I wonder how ever you live up here" or "I wouldn't be found dead up here", but we used to make our own fun and I think mebbe we were happier than they were. Everyone used to help each other.

'Sometimes if a man was having a bit of trouble trying to get his hay in during damp weather he'd find eighteen to twenty people in his field mucking in.

'And if any of the womenfolk wanted something special from Hawes all they had to do was ask the Harpers at Mouse Syke. Tom Harper had a trap and a gay, good horse and never missed going to Tuesday market at Hawes, unless it was too stormy to get out. Winter meant everybody would be trapped in regular, like, but the women would be ready for that. They'd stock in before with sacks of flour, forty to fifty stone of potatoes and anything else they might need.

'There was one winter when I was a lad when Grisedale was cut off for six weeks. In the end the farmers cut a way through themselves so that William Hodgson Harper could get his horse and wagon in. He used to leave everything at Moor Rigg and I remember my father going down there to bring provisions in. He bought a ten stone bag of flour one day, split it and carried it on his back up to our farm. Then after he finished work he went down for the other half. Then he would wait for the moonlit night and go down again to carry in oil cake for the calves!

'Normally, there wasn't much to do on winter nights and we children were always in bed at 7 p.m. We'd lie in bed listening to my father reading to mother. He would borrow books from my Uncle Jim, generally of religious type, and mother would listen as she darned socks and repaired trousers and such like.

'Mind, nothing was bought that could be made. All the bread, cheese and butter was home produced. And as many clothes as our mothers could manage. It was quite a problem, clothing, in our house with all those children. We'd have hard wearing corduroy trousers and jackets but woollen things didn't do so well with us. They'd be full of holes in no time. If it wasn't for my grandmother Mary Pratt who lived in Settle I don't know what my parents would have done about clothes. She was a tremendously good knitter, able to compete with the Dent knitters who were quite famous. I never saw anybody who could knit as fast as her. Mother and father would supply her with the wool and she knitted for us children for nothing. She could finish a pair of

Market day in the centre of Hawes at the turn of the century.

stockings in a day and still do all her housework. Always she was knitting, walking round the house and talking to you at the same time. She didn't even have to look down when she changed a needle from the band she wore round her apron.'

Wensleydale was full of furious knitters in the nineteenth century and they did not do it for fun. It was a measure of the poverty in which they lived that every opportunity and every moment had to be seized to try to make a little more money or save some. The wool from their sheep would be spun on frames in the house and hundreds of men, women and children carried their knitting wherever they went. Even the lead miners knitted as they walked miles through the darkness to the pit face. The people of Dent, which is just over the southern fell out of Garsdale were said to be the best and fastest knitters in the Dales and large bundles of socks and

Left: **Janet Harper who became Chris Pratt's wife.**
Right: **Chris and Janet Pratt in 1922.**

other woollen garments were carried each week to Hawes market by men and women who would be clicking assiduously away at next week's produce as they walked.

Being self-supporting and saving money were overriding considerations in Grisedale, where every natural resource was utilized to the full.

'We were lucky to have a lot of rushes growing on one swampy bit of Swarth Fell', recalls Chris Pratt. 'In the autumn everybody would be out mowing them and laying them in the barns because it meant we wouldn't have to buy straw for bedding the calves. A lot of time in the summer was spent cutting peat — we never used to burn anything else during the summer. Most people would be able to afford a few tons of coal for the winter but around the 1850s they even had their own coal mines on the eastern fell above High Flust, Fea Foe and East House.

'It was open cast mining, really, and the seam was about four inches thick. There are lots of shale heaps up there which have grown over now where the farmers kept digging until it was exhausted. They didn't sell it because they would need it for themselves in winter, particularly if the summer had been bad and there wasn't much peat stored. There had been a proper coal mine once in Cotterdale, a little valley off the road to Hawes, because my great-grandfather, James Brunskill and his father and brothers had been pitmen there when they lived at High Hall in Lunds. It was opened up again for a bit during the 1926 strike and I was sent to get a load to bring into Grisedale.'

Keeping warm in winter was not easy in Grisedale and a lot of serious illness was probably caused by damp and intense cold. Pneumonia was a common cause of death, and many families lost young children. Chris Pratt remembers the death of a sister six days after her birth and another weeks'-old child dying at Mouse Syke. Consumption, the old name for tuberculosis, was another killer.

'It was one of the scourges of Grisedale at the turn of the century. Quite a lot of young women died, including my wife's mother. That was in 1904 and she was only thirty. And I was told about a 17-year old girl dying in 1896. You only sent to Hawes for Dr Grimes if someone was seriously ill and there was no hospital to go to until the war years and then people were sent all the way to Bradford. Generally speaking, any illness that needed an operation was almost certain to be a killer.'

Even small accidents could lead to permanent maiming. Chris knew a man called Jack Atkinson who wore an eye patch after a minor accident with a knife blinded him in one eye, and Chris himself has one thumb missing.

'I cut it a little, only a touch, but it became so sore that I could hardly milk. Then it turned to blood poisoning and I had to have it off. There was no such thing as penicillin in them days.'

Sanitation was another problem in Grisedale. Earth closets were standard in Chris Pratt's day but Round Ing did not even have that facility until the Pratt's arrived. The previous tenant had used a wall in a field behind the house. Water had to be carried from springs.

'The landlord did build us an earth closet at the end of the house but it was a bit exposed and we'd often have to dig out a cartload of snow to get to it in winter. The door didn't fit too well and since you could see if anyone was coming you didn't bother to shut the door much. Anyway, if you did you'd have to get into the corner and put your shoulder behind it because it was so difficult.

'Only Scale had piped water. You see, Jack Dent had been a builder — he supervised the building of the Chapel — and he was a bit modern. He built a little wash house across from his farm and laid water to it. And a tap! It was the only tap in Grisedale. We had a zinc tin for bathing in at our place and our parents would wash us frequently when we were young. But we didn't have many baths when we got older.'

Grisedale largely escaped the health hazards inevitably presented by such primitive conditions, but there was one bad moment in 1916 when Richard Allen, the son of the Jim Allen converted by Dick Atkinson, died at East House of typhoid fever, aged thirty-six. Grisedale held its breath and long memories thought back to another fever which swept round the valley many years before.

'Aye, I knew an old man called Nathan Burton who lived in Lunds and he was always frightened of diptheria. He had been born in Grisedale and I remember him telling me that when he was a lad around 1860 there had been an epidemic of diptheria in the dale. He said seven people died.'

There was to be one last significant attempt at the end of the depressed thirties to inject new blood into the fast hardening arteries of Grisedale. It was made by a man in whom the spirit of old Grisedale still surges, who daily tramps its pastures and fells. He bears an honoured and familiar name in the valley: Pratt.

Dick Pratt was not born in the dale, nor was his father, Matthew, a cousin of Chris Pratt's father. They lived at a farm called East Mudbecks in Garsdale but Matthew had acquired the ownership of both Blake Mire and Aldershaw. When he died in 1938 he left Blake Mire to Dick, a bachelor of twenty-eight and keen to farm in his own right. Around the same time, old Mike Wilkinson, now on his own, decided to retire and leave. The new owner eagerly seized the chance to move in, pausing only to get married. But his bride did not share this enthusiasm. Bessie Miller had been born a farmer's daughter and could cope with all the jobs expected of a farmer's wife, but her father had died when she was still a small child and her mother moved to Hawes to run a guest house. So she was more of a town girl, accustomed to bustle and plenty of company.

'Before we got wed, Dick promised me that we would only spend two or three years there and then move on to a better place. There was no electricity, no tap and no road up to it — it took nearly fifteen minutes to get up the fields to the house. I went to have a look before we moved in and I thought it was a terrible place. This old man was sitting hunched up near the fire with a shawl round his shoulders and a dog at his feet.

The room had stone flag floors. It took me a month to get the place right, sleeping at Garsdale and going in every day with my friends to clean up. We must have burned at least thirty pairs of old clogs and boots. When the time came for us to move in I just didn't want to go.

'We ended up staying there for thirty years and I hated every minute of it. Those were supposed to be the best years of my life but you were buried alive there. I missed the company I had in Hawes, missed going to the church there. One winter I went for ten weeks without seeing anyone else.'

That was the winter of 1947, which is still talked about with awe throughout the Yorkshire Dales. It was the worst winter of the century up to now and it brought Grisedale to its knees. During the previous nine years Dick Pratt had done reasonably well, along with the survivors from the depression, for a war always elevates the status of farmers within society, as well as the prices for their produce. It is clear that the Second World War prolonged the life of old Grisedale. Clearly, too, Dick was enchanted with the place and could not bear to leave. Bessie had given birth to a daughter, Audrey, in 1941 and a son, John, in 1945, and was busy being a traditional Grisedale housewife, churning butter to sell and carrying water from the spring. Dick had sixty-five acres of enclosed land for his thirty-five cattle, had two good Dales horses and a healthy slice of the fells to keep his hardy Swaledale sheep, which had bred up to around 250 head when 1947 dawned. And then the storm broke.

'It started on January 24th, freezing and blowing snow hard. When the middle of February arrived and it hadn't stopped we realized we were in for a bad one. Luckily I had a dog called Moss which could find sheep buried anywhere, even when they were ten or twelve feet under the snow. So we got them dug out and gathered in behind the barn for shelter. But the snow got worse and worse, piling up as high as the house. We never saw the stone walls and gates for weeks and could drive straight over the top of them with a horse. Watering the cattle and horses was a real problem. The usual place they drank at was frozen over and hidden for weeks and weeks but we had a spring that never freezes fifty yards down a field. So I got busy and cut a track down to it and then dug down to find it. I put an old door across to stop the snow blowing back and led them all down every day and lifted buckets of water out so they could drink. Those poor beasts were so thirsty they would follow me up that track with no trouble and go back on their

Opposite: **Chris Pratt, molecatcher.**

own after they'd had enough. You know, it was so cold that it would freeze the clothes stiff on your back. When I came in from work and took off my topcoat it would stand straight up on its own. It was the cold that killed most of the sheep, not shortage of food, although I did find ten smothered to death in a heap under a drift one morning. You see, they would huddle very close together behind the barn and start sweating. Then they would open out and die from pneumonia. Getting food to them wasn't the main problem because they dropped hay to us from the air. Mind, they nearly bombed us out of house and home on one occasion. I was working round the farmhouse that day with a German prisoner of war called Hans Vieten who had been sent to work for us. He spoke broken English, and suddenly he spotted a plane coming from the direction of the Moorcock. He shouted out: "Hey there, farmer up Dale. Hey, him very low — Moorcock", and pointed at the plane. Well, this plane dropped a bale right through our roof, sending the slates flying into the air. And our John who was only two, was asleep upstairs. The missus came running out shouting "Stop him, stop him, stop him", and I said: "How the hell can I stop him with him up there". But the German prisoner shouted: "ja, ja, me stop him, me stop him" and he ran out into the field and started giving signals to the pilot with his arms. We just stood and stared. Anyway, it worked perfectly because the pilot dropped two more bales of hay in a straight line within a hundred yards of the house. It turned out that Hans had been a paratrooper dropped behind the Russian lines to fight and had lived for three months on supplies dropped by plane. There must have been an international code which the pilot understood.

'But the hay didn't help much with the sheep. It kept snowing right into April and when the thaw came we had to dig channels round the house to stop it being flooded. But the sheep were so weak they would drown trying to jump the beck. They had no flesh on them and when lambing time came they hadn't the strength to get rid of the lamb. I lost nearly 150 sheep and there was no lamb crop to speak of — about 40 we finished up with instead of 200. At least we got a bit of assistance from the government who paid us fifty per cent of the value lost, but that wasn't the same as having your fell bred sheep.'

But Dick Pratt's losses were minor compared to the crippling blow sustained by the man who was farming East House in 1947. He had only taken over the tenancy at the back end of 1946 and was not experienced in hill farming. He brought with him two large and heavy low-country horses, mostly Clydesdale, and a herd of cattle, and took over 150 ewes and fifty gimmer hogs (first year sheep) already hardened to Grisedale. When spring came he had thirty-eight ewes and twelve gimmer hogs left and his lamb crop was a pitiful nineteen. Almost half a dozen of his cattle died, too, and both his horses, which were not bred to stand cold like that. They just slumped down and could not get up. Naturally he left for a kinder environment.

Altogether, more than five hundred sheep perished in Grisedale during that killing winter — approximately half the total. When all the snow had gone a party of sixteen German prisoners of war were brought into the dale by lorry each day with shovels. They dug a large hole for each farm so that Grisedale's dead could be decently buried. The bodies were brought in by horse and cart.

'The prisoners came from a camp at Milnthorpe and they had to stay behind a bit after the war was finished. One trusty was allocated to each farm and if we were well satisfied with them they were allowed to stay. We liked our lad, Hans, tremendous well and when the time came for him to go back to Germany I asked him to stay. Well, he was delighted and stopped for another year. He got his civilian clothes and a civilian wage, too.'

Grisedale declined rapidly after 1947. Aldershaw was already empty before Dick Pratt came to Blake Mire, and he watched sadly as farm after farm was abandoned. The death of a farm was .

Chris Pratt by the ruins of Round Ing.

Chris Pratt at Hawes Junction Chapel.

usually preceded by several quick changes of ownership as new and unfamiliar names came briefly into Grisedale and then thought better of it. Jack and Maggie Thwaite stuck it out at Mouse Syke and Bob Thornborrow, son of the Fea Foe family which had befriended Rose Harper, tried his luck at Moor Rigg. The ownership of Round Ing reverted to Chris Pratt but he was not prepared to live there any more. He rented the house to old Dick Harper and ran some sheep on the land, walking in from Garsdale to tend them. Twelve of them were buried under an amazing twenty foot drift in 1947 and they were finally dug out just before midnight, with the aid of blazing Tilley lamps. A year later Round Ing was left empty, never to be occupied again.

Scale, which has an interesting spiral staircase in one of the outbuildings which is considered to be of historical value, was vacated about a year later and began tumbling down quickly. Moor Rigg followed and was left to the mercy of the weather for ten years until it was converted into two cottages. Fea Foe was abandoned towards the end of the fifties. But the local Methodists grimly kept Grisedale's chapel open, holding regular services until August 1970. Only then did they admit that the Richard Atkinson Memorial Wesleyan Chapel was really just a memorial — to a long departed community. Sentiment brought old Grisedalians and their descendants flocking back to the dale for the final service, some travelling many miles, and extra forms had to be carried in to seat everyone for this emotional occasion. Then the memorial stone in the gable end facing the dale was prised out and re-erected in the graveyard of one of the four Methodist chapels in Garsdale. The following year, after a decent interval, the building was sold and converted into a weekend cottage.

In 1961, the twentieth century in the shape of the North Eastern Electricity Board unexpectedly discovered the existence of Grisedale and came to offer power. But it was too late. Bessie Pratt, whose dislike of Blake Mire had not diminished with the years, and Dick accepted with delight but Jack Thwaite at Mouse Syke announced that he was very happy with Calor gas and politely showed the N.E.E.B. salesmen the door. East House and Moor Rigg also declined.

By 1968, farming had ceased at East House and Dick Pratt and Jack Thwaite were the last remaining farmers living in Grisedale. And in that year Bessie Pratt decided that thirty years was just about as long as she could take at Black Mire. The tenancy of Dick Atkinson's old house, Grouse Hall, still occupied by the local gamekeeper, came free.

'I didn't even think twice. I went straight there and took it, without my husband's consent. He wanted to stay at Black Mire but I said I was going to Grouse Hall whatever he did, that's the truth! So he very reluctantly came, but later on he admitted that he was very pleased with the place. It was winter and we brought our furniture out of Blake Mire on a sledge. In fact, it was January 22nd, 1968, because I wrote in my diary: "This is the happiest day of my life!" '

One who always shared Dick Pratt's enthusiasm for Grisedale was his son, John. Whilst his daughter, Audrey, now married, was happy to go to boarding school and escape the inevitable loneliness for a child, Bessie never did have any similar worries about her son.

'John always relished the place. He still loves it. There were no pals for him really but he didn't seem to mind. He used to go up on the fells by himself at a very early age and he knew every sheep. One of his favourite games was to play with marbles and he would even pretend they were sheep. So we let him go to the Chapel School in Garsdale and he used to walk there until they got a van as school transport.'

John is thirty, unmarried and totally absorbed with Grisedale. Like his father he is an expert horseman, and breeds Fell ponies which would have delighted old Dalesmen. Ten of them now wheel and gallop around the empty fells.

'I suppose I did have a lonely childhood but then I had two dogs of my own, Gyp and Mist, and

I was always interested in sheep and horses, as long as I can remember. Not cows, just sheep and fell ponies. Even when I was very young I'd go up to the fell on my pony with the dogs and practise gathering sheep.'

His father, too, is still a Grisedalian at heart. When he strode glumly down to Grouse Hall he sold the farmhouse at Blake Mire as a country retreat to a publisher in London but refused to part with the land. He then set about collecting the ruins of old Grisedale with relentless passion. Round Ing, High Ing and Scale are now his and he rents Fea Foe. Altogether he owns over 400 acres, a lot of millstone grit and the right to graze his large flock of sheep over a sizable proportion of the fells. Every day he and his son leave Grouse Hall and are swallowed by the fells and pastures of Grisedale until the light goes.

The memorial stone from the Richard Atkinson Memorial Chapel taken from Grisedale and erected in Garsdale.

Enter Joe Gibson

IN the summer of 1969 it appeared that the one slender strand that linked Grisedale back through a thousand vivid years to the Viking founding fathers was about to break. The Thwaites, lone guardians of the valley's heritage, left for Sedbergh and retirement after an uninterrupted thirty-nine years at the single remaining farm. Will Airey and his wife, Mary, and two children, came to take over Mouse Syke and the attendant responsibility. Almost immediately, Will was offered another, more attractive tenancy outside the dale and took it. He handed in his notice and started to pack.

It seemed to be all over for Grisedale, and everything it stood for. But loping over the fell road which plunges into the valley came a curious figure with an unusual gait and an armful of books. Even at a distance an experienced eye could tell that Joe Gibson was no Dalesman, for hillfolk have a distinct style of movement born of centuries of fell walking, and a considered way of speech and gesture. Nevertheless, Joe also came from a peculiar breed of men with equally pronounced characteristics. Like his ancestors, he was more accustomed to hacking and heaving a mile underground than to chasing sheep at 2,500 feet above sea level. He had been a miner in Seghill, Northumberland, for more than a quarter of a century.

But with the confidence of his indomitable breed, he breezed into Mouse Syke with his wife and began studying those books he carried in very closely indeed. He had bought them in Newcastle and they advised the reader how to raise hill sheep and beef cattle, and how to become your own vet. The Dalesmen around Upper Wensleydale considered this strange situation very carefully, listened to his oddly musical accent, inquired into his background, discovered he was almost sixty and shook their heads sadly. An emissary came down to Mouse Syke and delivered the widely agreed verdict. Joe grins widely as he remembers the words exactly.

'He said to me that Grisedale could ruin me in one year. You have to know these hill sheep, he said. It just needs one hard winter and you'll lose every penny.'

But fighting against heavy odds has been the very stuff of Joe Gibson's life since he was a young man. Before he was sixteen he went down the pit, which would not be permitted today. He never did like working underground and over a period of thirty years made valiant but unsuccessful attempts to break free, and live in the fresh, clean air.

'Being a pitman wasn't the sort of life I wanted at all. I never did take to all that boozing, baccy and betting, and what's more I had the nastiest job in the mine. I had to take the timbers out and let the roof down as the face advanced 4 feet 6 inches every day. That takes the weight off the face, you see. It meant I was causing a collapse every time I went down and I had a few near dos. Once I broke a leg and another time a shelf came down right on top of me and covered me completely. I thought the whole lot had gone but I got out all right. My mate used to say to me that if the insurance man could see us down there he'd take us straight off his books. So I looked for a way out and eventually started a radio battery charging business. Very few houses in Seghill had electricity in those days but mine was one so I left the pit and opened up for business in a wooden hut. We took our supply from the colliery and we did very well at first. In fact, we were charging 1,500 batteries a week at one time and we put such a load on the system that the village supply used to drop from 220 to 160 volts! The lights in the street used to go very dim in winter time, I'll tell you. Anyway, after a bit the whole village was electrified and that killed it. I had to go back to the pit.

'Eventually I got another opportunity to break out. We had one of the best and biggest houses in Seghill, a semi-detached which my wife, Jenny and I saved hard for and managed to buy for £800. Well, the Coal Board came looking for a good place to buy for one of their officials and they offered me £1,200, which was a fantastic price in 1956. Now I'd thought that a petrol-filling station might do well in the village because miners were starting to earn enough to afford cars. I got an option on a nice bit of land and applied for permission to build a bungalow and a garage. But it took five sets of plans and two years before we finally got the go-ahead. So the Coal Board could have the house I bought a caravan and we lived in that on the site. Then we set to on the bungalow and I did a deal with two bricklayers to put the shell up. Apart from them the only other people I paid were the slaters and the plasterers. Me and my mates did all the rest, digging the foundations, the drains, laying the roads, doing the joinery, plumbing and electrical work. We started at Easter and finished by December. All this time I was still working at the pit, building the bungalow by day, going on the night shift at 5 p.m. and getting back at 2 a.m. But when it came to starting the garage I had run out of money. I didn't know what to do but my accountant said: "Joe, just get on and build it and don't pay the bills." So I did, built it every bit myself. There are 22,000 bricks in that garage and I laid each one.'

Joe had escaped once more. The garage opened, the bills were paid and bringing the roof down for a living was in the past. Or so it looked for three years.

'Three years, and that was it. I thought I had a real going concern and then they went and started to close down the mines. The lads began selling their cars instead of buying petrol. Everything declined, including my garage, so in 1961 I sold out. But I'd decided I wasn't going back down there again.'

His next decision astonished everyone, particularly Jenny Gibson, who had struggled by his side all through the difficult times, bringing up a son and a daughter.

'He thought about things for a while and then one day announced that he was going to get a farm. Just like that. And we climbed into the car and went looking for farms all over the place, right the way down to Keighley and Hebden Bridge. Later on he spotted an advertisement in the *Newcastle Journal* for a farm in Sedbergh and we agreed to take it. We even moved in but we didn't actually buy it because a better one came up for sale in Cautley. Since the owner was a relative of the man with the first farm we were able to arrange the switch.'

Joe's satisfaction in moving to the Yorkshire Dales from an ugly mining area and setting up as a farmer was soon to be disturbed. His experience of farming was limited to helping on a pig farm for a month or two just after leaving school, and thirty-nine acres must have appeared like a prairie to him after Seghill. But it was not big enough for a dairy farm. Joe built up his herd to eighteen but he could not make enough to live on from the farm alone. And the man who had once owned his own garage was forced to seek a job at a garage in Sedbergh. Joe was no longer a young man and this was the third time fate had slapped him hard in the face. Anyone less

Opposite: **Joe Gibson and his dogs in Grisedale.**

accustomed to fighting back would have capitulated, but Joe thought hard as he sweated with cylinder heads and grease guns during the day and cows udders at dawn and dusk.

'And then it occurred to me — a caravan site! So I got permission, sold the cows and opened up for business once again. It worked. We became a very popular place for holidaymakers.'

But the urge to become a farmer in the fullest sense had not deserted Joe, and fate now began to push him towards his true destiny. He relentlessly cast around once more for a farm, a real farm this time, and in 1968 he found out that a tenancy was coming vacant in an odd little place called Grisedale.

'We came up and had a look. It was the idea of all that land that attracted me. Why, there were 257 acres and a portion of the fells as well. All those acres! After Will Airey had decided to leave no one else appeared to be interested, so we took it. You see, I knew I'd never be able to afford to buy a place that big but if I sold the farm and caravan site at Cautley I'd have enough to stock it up. I got £6,000 for Cautley, which was £2,500 more than we paid for it, although we'd put water in and started the caravans.'

Under the gloomy gaze of established hill farmers in the area, Joe and Jenny came into Mouse Syke and took over 120 ewes and 40 hogs already resident. Joe was a little over five years away from becoming a pensioner, his living room was 1,120 feet above sea level and he had never owned a sheep before. At least there was electricty, which the owners installed just before the Gibsons arrived. Joe added some fell hardened Aberdeen Angus and Hereford cattle to his stock and bought essential machinery and a tractor. He was ready to go.

'I had some luck with the weather. There hasn't been a really bad winter since we arrived so I've never had a big loss. I read my books and learned some other things from experience, such as how to find buried sheep. You get to know where they shelter when the blizzards come and if you look carefully you'll find a little hole in the snow, no bigger than your finger. That's an air hole and if you dig down you'll find a sheep, or maybe two or three together. I've tracked down and rescued scores like that — thirty-four in a day last year — and never lost one. In fact, I've never had more than five sheep die in a year and they were usually old ewes.

'I learned about training sheepdogs from a book, too. I borrowed a really good one from a young chap and found out how to do the right whistle, the drive whistle and the gather whistle. You can learn just about anything from the right book, you know. Now I've got two working dogs and a pup coming up and whilst they're not a patch on some of the dogs round here at least I can gather my sheep with them.'

Joe's relationship with the faintly astonished old Dalesman watching his progress has always been friendly, but warmth was slow to develop. No off-comer has ever been accepted quickly and without reservation in the more remote Dales. Joe, accustomed to the unique *camaraderie* of the pit where danger and darkness quickly forge deep friendships, found the new climate curious.

'They were always pleasant, right from the start. But to get right down and know a person really intimately is another matter here. Back home there was no hanging back, no ifs and buts. But Dalesmen are very careful before they speak out. It's just their nature, you see. At first when I had a problem and sought some advice I'd go to a fellow and say: "I've got a sheep which walks a few yards and then falls down—what do you think it could be then?" And he'd say "Oh, it could be this or it could be that" and then just leave you. I think they're afraid to give you advice in case it goes wrong. That's just what happened once when someone out of Sedbergh came to look at one of my lambs that was ailing and said I should give it half a pint of milk with a fresh egg beaten in. I told him to go ahead and he picked the lamb up and poured this stuff down its throat. Two

Joe and Chris Pratt by the ruins of Reacher.

Above: Lambing time in Joe's beloved Grisedale.
Opposite: Joe and Jenny Gibson happily at work with their sheep in the 1970s.

minutes later it was dead. Back at Cautley I had a cow that was badly, and one old character told me that the best thing was to get a handful of soil from the ground under a hazel tree and push it down its throat. I resisted that one.

'But now I've been in Grisedale five years I feel I've been accepted. I mix in with them down at Hawes market now like one of them. In fact, my neighbours are marvellous when I'm in trouble. In 1973 I had to go into hospital in Lancaster for an operation to remove gall stones and I came back to find that all my hay was in and all my sheep clipped.'

Jenny Gibson was also overwhelmed by the generosity of Grisedale when Joe had to leave her to manage for a fortnight.

'There were three Pratts all shearing Joe's sheep at the same time. One of them even paid someone else to do his so he could come here, but he refused to let us hire the same man. And someone turned up in a car every day for a fortnight, never missing a day, to drive me forty miles to Lancaster and forty miles back so I could see Joe. That's what you call neighbours.'

This acceptance of the Gibsons was hastened by their devotion to the Methodist cause. Most Sundays will find Joe in one of the pulpits of Upper Wensleydale, where he preaches a fine, incisive sermon. For half a decade the savage face of Grisedale has not presented itself to Joe, but he has not been lulled into believing that the run of mild winters will go on for ever. As he says, Grisedale could be preparing to give him a 'real good clout' any time. In fact, he came close to disaster when the atrocious summer of 1974 prevented him from getting any hay crop at all. At the same time, the price of hay at the merchant's rocketed from £20 to £60 a ton. In common with hundreds of other small farmers, Joe might have been bankrupted if the winter of 1975 had been a bad one, demanding constant fodder for his sheep and cattle. But when February came and went benignly and March dawned brightly with the sheep still getting all the grass they needed, the crisis was almost over. Hay prices slumped, too, and when Joe went into hospital again at the end of February for another gallstone operation he chanced to meet a farmer who had a ton of hay he did not want. It's now in the barn of Mouse Syke, delivered by one of his friends rallying round again.

The Gibsons radiate a deep contentment with their lives in Grisedale. Joe now has time to develop his talent for painting and his wild Grisedalian landscapes are exhibited at the Sedbergh Arts Society. Two have been sold. Jenny busies herself round their bright and attractive house and bakes delicious buns and pies in the classic Wensleydale tradition. And now she has a grandson to fuss over when their son and daughter-in-law make their frequent visits. The life they disliked so much in the pit village is firmly behind them, although Joe did have an unpleasant reminder of the hazards he once faced every day when a gable end of an outbuilding at Mouse Syke tumbled when he was attempting some alterations.

'It had a few tons of stone, too, did that gable end. These places were built without cement, you know, and I was trying to move a door when it went. But I saw it coming and got out of the way.'

At times like lambing and shearing, Joe and Jenny work shoulder to shoulder on the pastures and fells, both totally absorbed in the fascination of farming, of supervising the creation of new life and the continuance of old crafts and revelling in the application of their rural skills. The transformation of Jenny into a farmer's wife surprised herself more than anyone.

Opposite: **Joe Gibson with a drowned sheep in Grisedale.**

Above: **The spirit of lonely Grisedale.**
Opposite: **Joe Gibson — landscape painter.**

'That day back in Seghill when Joe decided to be a farmer, I said to him: "Joe, I'll come with you but I'm not farming." And now I say to him: "Why didn't you have this idea when we were younger."'

As for Joe, who keeps a miner's lamp hanging by the fireside as a symbol of the life he escaped, he declares:

'You are nearer to hell in a pit than anywhere else on earth. And at my time of life I wanted to be as close to Heaven as I can get.'

But there is one flaw in this happy state. The Gibsons' desire to live out the rest of their lives in Grisedale is not absolutely assured of fulfilment, which means that the last vestige of Grisedale's past glory is threatened anew. Their son, David, shares his father's passion for the place and when Joe took the tenancy he says he tried to put Mouse Syke in both their names to ensure succession.

'But they wouldn't do that. They said it was the custom in the estate farms for son to follow father. But the agent who told me that has gone now and the new man has talked to me about selling Mouse Syke. In fact, he wanted me to set a date for retirement, although I have security of tenure until I die. The price he has mentioned for the place is very high — in the region of £25,000. I can't possibly afford that and neither can David. He's working away on civil engineering projects, laying oil pipelines down from Scotland, but he and his wife are keen to come here. I don't know what will happen. But we are determined to stay, to the end. I've even said that I'll have a cardboard cut-out of myself so that when I die they can prop that up at the window to kid everybody that I'm still alive!'

So Joe faces up to the future once more with a fight on his hands. But now he fights not just for himself and his family, but for the very spirit of all the lost generations of Grisedale. He has evolved a typically bold idea. Plans have been drawn up and outline planning permission granted for the building of a home in Grisedale. For Joe has acquired the ruins of Aldershaw and he and David intend to take the scattered heaps of darkly weathered stone with their bare hands and rebuild them. If they succeed, it will be the first home built in the dale for more centuries than anyone can recall.

A moving declaration of faith in Grisedale which will earn the unreserved support of the ghosts of Richard Atkinson and his kind, the spirits of the Vikings in Valhalla and everyone who cares for the golden thread of continuity which more than anything else makes the Dales of Yorkshire such an inspirational place.

Postscript

JOE GIBSON won his battle in the end — but at a price.

His wife, Jenny, died in 1979 and that blow, coupled with the severe winter which followed, led to Joe leaving Grisedale. But Mouse Syke is still, happily, in the hands of the Gibsons. His son, David, took over and in 1981 was even able to buy the place.

You can imagine the intense satisfaction that gave Joe.

Several of the ruins have been restored as holiday homes and ten dwellings now flourish in Grisedale — a further tribute to this indomitable ex-miner, since it was his lone struggle to breathe life into the valley that brought it to the attention of the world outside.

Joe remarried and eventually headed North East towards his roots. Now in his late seventies, he and Ada live in retirement in Darlington.

Chris Pratt also died in 1979 — altogether a very sad year for Grisedale. But the other resolute branch of the Pratt family at Grouse Hall have added more acres to their Grisedale property and keep tradition triumphantly alive and well.

The Ways of a Yorkshire Dale

Ironstone Joe

JOE SUNLEY is built from the ironstone which his father mined with a great bitterness. There are no compromises in life for this small and slightly stooped man with hair so gleaming white that it stands like a heliograph when he is half a mile down his fields. Joe has a charisma which radiates with even greater strength. He deliberates every point with the gravity of a high court judge and he rules his farm at Girrick, down a narrow lane off the road betwen Guisborough and Whitby, without making many concessions to what most people accept as a normal lifestyle.

Joe's mother and father brought up five sons and two daughters at 195 Westgate, Guisborough. His father was a time-serving blacksmith but was obliged to give up this dignified trade and go into the iron ore mines which proliferated round the Guisborough area to earn the larger rewards dangled by the pit masters. His hatred of this work is clear in the ringing declaration he issued to his sons:

"I will take an axe and chop off your hands rather than let any of you go down a pit."

None of them ever did.

The iron ore mines are all closed now, leaving behind the painful memory and a range of conical shale tips. One of the largest sticks out like a boil on the bottom of the otherwise beautiful vista from Joe's farm. His fields appear to fall into the creamy embrace of the sea.

Sunley senior was a man of principle. He did not take the quickest way out of his misery like so many of his fellow miners, who spent a substantial proportion of their wages drowning their sorrows every week. Indeed, he was never known to get drunk. He insisted that his family wore leather boots, not clogs like all the others, and three-quarters of his money was spent on food.

'My father believed very strongly in us being shod with leather and keeping our bellies full,' says Joe. 'He had two sayings: "If your boots and hair are clean, you're half dressed" and "Back will trust, but belly won't." '

Life was still harsh for the Sunleys, particularly for the young Joe who caught diptheria. It left a permanent mark on him.

'I was in a sanatorium for six months and I was left very weak. So to strengthen my legs I was sent to a school two miles away and I had to walk there and back every day. These days parents would be crying for a bus but mine were just the opposite and I think they were right.'

This kind of philosophy endures almost undiminished to this day at Joe's farm. The way of life there is probably unique in this country for its remorseless work cycle—up at 6 a.m. bring in the cows, milk by hand for three hours, swill out the byres and clean up the yard; have breakfast of cereal, hot milk, crackers, bread and tea. Then take out the cows, stack the bales of hay in the farm, manhandle the churns to the top of the road for collection, cut the grass, harvest the corn, play mid-wife to a pregnant cow; break for lunch at around 3.30 p.m., back out again to feed the horses, mend the fences, hack down the thistles, and work on until the cows come home again for another three hours of hauling away at their udders. Every day for sixteen hours, until nine at night and sometimes beyond. One hundred and twenty-six man (and woman) hours per week are spent milking, a job which could be done mechanically and in a fraction of the time if Joe had agreed to the intrusion of electricity.

If work is good for the soul, then Joe, his wife Connie, and daughter Mary, are angels for sure.

But for Joe these hours are perfectly normal—he has always worked them, by and large. As a lad he rose at six, weakling or not, and ran to Guisborough railway station to pick up a bundle of newspapers which he then delivered round the town before going to school. The newsagent, a Mr. Gill, was also a barber and the job, which paid two shillings and sixpence a week, also embraced the duties of lather-boy.

'We always worked until nine at night on Saturdays. There were four chairs and Mr. Gill charged fourpence for a haircut and twopence for a shave. He could shave 'em as fast as I could lather 'em. Every Saturday night without fail just as the clock was striking nine and we were supposed to be shutting up shop a fishmonger would come in for a shave. I think he must have lived on fish that was going off because the stench from him was always horrible. He used to sit back in the chair and open his mouth wide, and I longed to get the biggest brush of lather I could and jam it in.

When he left school he went to work in a bakery, greasing tins and washing up, starting once again at 6 a.m. and working a twelve-hour day. His pay was three shillings a week and he was allowed to keep threepence for himself. At the age of fourteen, ready for man's work, he was apprenticed as a fitter and turner at the local foundry for six shillings a week, with a shilling rise every six months.

Joe and his family did not go to church with the rest of the crowd because his mother was a 'bit of a rebel' when it came to religion. 'She'd been tanned as a girl for not curtsying to the parson and this incident did not enamour her of the church,' says Joe. 'So I went to the Salvation Army because it was reckoned they did a bit of good. But when General Booth died and there was a big row over the million pounds he had collected from pennies on the drum I became a choirboy at the Parish Church. My pal was in the choir so I applied for an audition, with my parents' permission, and was accepted.'

Joe's romance with the established church did not, however, survive what he calls a 'broken promise.' Apparently the parson stopped the choir trips during the First World War, which led to a deputation asking for a resumption of this much coveted annual treat.

'He said there would be the best trip there had ever been when the war was over but it never happened.'

Joe is still a religious rebel, adhering to a set of beliefs which are exceedingly harsh when compared to the accepted norm. He is not liked for these views in some quarters of East Cleveland society but he never flinches from criticism. He says he is not religious in the formal sense, just lives 'by the Bible.' But for around two decades he has generally followed the dictum of the Jehovah's Witnesses sect, which is only for disciplinarians. Birthdays are not celebrated because the only two birthdays mentioned in the Bible were those of evil men. Christmas is not kept because the word from the Watchtower says Christ was born almost three months before December 25th.

Yet there was once a time for Joe when life was sweet and wholesome and he was not troubled by the sinfulness of men . . . when Connie walked into his life with a packet of sandwiches. She was seventeen then and a lass who would turn any young man's head as she walked along

Opposite: **Joe Sunley looks carefully over one of his horses.**

Applegarth, the Sunday afternoon parade ground for the young people of Guisborough. Connie had a friend who used to take tea to her father at the foundry, so she went with her one day and met Joe, who was then twenty-one and no longer a raw apprentice. They walked Applegarth together, and then the winding lanes to Connie's home three miles out of town. They became so wrapped up in each other that their walks went on for sixteen miles and more on those blissful Sundays of their youth.

Alas, their dreams of marriage and a home together were shattered by a double blow. Joe's father was invalided out of the mines with bronchitis and Joe, the eldest son, had to shoulder the responsibility of being the family's main breadwinner. And Connie's father died at the age of forty-nine. The Saturday following the funeral Connie, an only child, and her mother were obliged to get out of their house. Mother took a position as housekeeper and Connie went into service, working twelve hours a day for four shillings and sixpence a week.

For seven long years they courted, and walked, and waited. But instead of getting better, things got worse. Joe's mother died, and in 1931 he was made redundant. Two years later he was still out of work—and the unemployed received the dole for only the first six months in those black days of the Depression.

'By then I was twenty-eight you see, and I decided it was time to do something about getting married. So I had a talk with my father and he agreed that I had my own life to lead. Although I had no job I was turning my hand to anything that came along, growing food on two allotments, putting windows in for twice the price of the glass, anything. We went house hunting but no one would let me one as I was out of work. Then I met a man who had been a foreman joiner at the place where I'd been employed. He'd set up on his own, building houses, and he said he'd sell me one. I told him I hadn't got the money. He offered to lend me the deposit if I could get a mortgage, so I went bravely to the Halifax Building Society offices and faced the manager. He decided to trust me, too, so we started married life in a brand new house with £2.5s. a month to find for the mortgage and no job!'

A desperate situation, and Joe turned naturally for a solution to the land, the source of life for his kind for over a millennium. His grandfather had been a farmer and three of his brothers went to work on farms. He began to work his two allotments commercially and sought opportunities to get into the milk business.

'I thought to myself . . . well, lad, industry's done with you and you've done with it. I'll have a go at agriculture. I started to grow cabbages and if we had more than we could sell locally I'd sell 'em to the greengrocers. Eight pence a dozen, big-hearted cabbages. I got some poultry and a pig and then I swapped a portable gramophone for a goat, which meant I was in the milk business. It's surprising, but a good goat will give a gallon of milk. Word got around and people offered me more goats because everyone was on the make for a bob or two then—you had to, or else you couldn't live. All I could give to my wife for housekeeping when we first got married was eight shillings a week. Then we managed to acquire a cow. I put five pounds down and paid it off at a pound a month. The price was eighteen pounds, which is laughable today. But we had a big setback after we'd had her a year. I ordered some flake maize but I wasn't there when the chap delivered it and he just dumped it in the building where she was kept. The cow got loose and she bust herself on it. Died. So I was back where I started.'

The memory of that disaster still touches a nerve with Connie.

'We'd had to work so hard and save so hard,' she says, with feeling. 'It put us down on our knees. When one cow was all you had it was a serious matter.'

Joe's fighting spirit was not quenched, however, and he had another piece of luck when a businessman heard about the misfortune and asked if he knew where he could get another cow. Joe told him he could get one for fifteen pounds.

'Well, I can see you're trying, lad,' he said. 'I'll lend you the fifteen pounds at six per cent, to be paid back over a year.'

Joe was away again. However, he had a debt to pay, and just how hard that was can be judged from the fact that this immensely proud man still had not paid it off at the end of the year. He had to obtain a month's extension. But he would turn his hand to anything. When the weather was warm, he and Connie worked laboriously to make ice-cream with the milk in a hand-cranked machine to sell on the streets of Guisborough and earn a few more coppers. The cow was kept in a henhouse on one of the allotments and Joe had to dig drains to satisfy the requirements of the local council, who sent their surveyor, the sanitary inspector and the medical officer to make sure that all by-laws had been complied with.

Hay for the cow was another major problem. Joe had no fields so he went out into the lanes with a scythe and cut the sides. When he built up his herd and began to breed heifers, getting enough hay became a tremendous burden.

'I got permission from the council to mow some of their land. And I went round offering to cut big lawns if I could keep the grass. I used to get several tons eventually, but it was a slow painful job.'

The sight of this grimly determined man carrying his scythe around the district searching for spare grass is still remembered. Sometimes, it is said, he was so tired at the end of the day that he scarcely had the strength to wrench his scythe free if the point jabbed into the ground.

He served a six-year apprenticeship to agriculture in this way and then in 1939 the established farming community accepted him. He was given the tenancy of Grange Farm, Girrick. Joe, Connie and their growing family marched eagerly down the narrow lane which slopes down to their farm accompanied by seven head of cattle, a few pigs and hens, less than one hundred pounds of capital but unlimited courage. Joe became the master of eighty acres of cold unfriendly land. The soil was not good. 'Never sow anything at Girrick before the second week in April,' was the advice offered.

Three decades later, the farm had fifty head of Jersey cows giving six churns of superb milk every day and his land was embellished with the spectacle of sixteen Cleveland Bay horses and gangling foals running thunderously free over his rolling acres in a way that would have excited the late Sir Alfred Munnings. Nothing else changed. The buildings remained much as they were a hundred years before Joe came, apart from an asbestos roofed shed. But that is how Joe likes it, for he is another who has no love for the tide of progress. There are few aids to modern living to ease the frugality of Grange Farm. Life generally is kept as it was in the past. Like other farmers, Joe was offered electricity but he turned it down. 'I like to keep things as simple as possible. Why make life any more complicated than it is! If we weren't milking by hand we'd only be doing something else. There's always a job looking at you on a farm. You could spend forty-eight hours every day and the work still wouldn't be done. Milking is quite a relaxing job, you know, and it gives you plenty of time to think. My mind goes round most problems, about everything in the world I should think.'

Connie, now in her sixties, clearly has a warmer opinion of electricity, but is hesitant to voice it strongly in deference to the master of the house.

'I had it all to leave when we came here. It took some doing, I can tell you. Electricity would be nice in a lot of ways, like for washing and things such as that. It's hard you know. I do all my washing by hand. But it's no good unless you're both of the same mind and we've managed all these years without it.

'Mind, it was worse than it is now, before we got the Calor gas. I had to heat the water for washing in the kitchen back boiler and I couldn't get it all done in one day then because I was washing for seven of us. We had five children in the house, you see.

'The hardest time we had came in the war because we had such a lot to do. We were obliged to grow corn and potatoes — oh, we were growing all the time there was and we got very tired. Then the children got up a bit and they started to help.

'But I was alright because I've had good health up to now. It doesn't bother me getting up at six o'clock and now most of the family's married I'd be lost if I didn't have outside work to do. Well, there's nothing else to do, really, because we can't get out much. There isn't the time.'

Obviously, Joe was a strict father to his children. They still all regard him with awe, even those who are married with homes and children of their own. Joe says he applied those stern principles of his by setting an example and having Bible readings when time permitted. He claims that he did not impose his views on them, he just told them 'what was right'. About corporal punishment he declares:

'You know what it says in the Good Book — spare the rod and spoil the child. If you beat them, they won't die. The rod of correction drives the foolishness from them. Apply those principles and you can't go far wrong.'

Sunley's Daughter

JOE SUNLEY'S daughter Mary is a delicate, spindly roe-deer of a girl, as shy as any wild creature of the fields. The world outside her father's farm has touched her so little that casual communication is almost impossible. She has been nowhere, experienced little, has no friends.

She goes about life with a strained, preoccupied look, and well she might. Her father is now an old man with failing strength and despite her slight stature, Mary has to shoulder the main burden of work. But she does it willingly, for her loyalty to her parents transcends everything. She is extremely attractive. Indeed, on the occasions when her cares melt away for a fleeting moment, she smiles and displays a startling beauty.

Mary Sunley is a prisoner of circumstance. She is the last child of the Sunley's — all the others, including her twin brother, have left Grange Farm to lead their own lives. If Mary went, the pattern of work on the farm would collapse. Even Joe would admit this. Mary is honouring a Dales tradition, which has resisted change in East Cleveland more than in any other rural area, that one child must stay behind to care for the ageing parents. Usually it is the youngest daughter, or the last daughter to win a man. This has led to some tragic situations in years gone by, repeated at least once in recent memory, when a man died aged well into his fifties. The funeral was attended by the grief-stricken figure of a maiden lady, his fiancée for more than twenty years.

In these Dales, it was once usual for a man to start carving marriage spoons when his proposal was accepted by his lady love. He would select a very long piece of wood and begin by carving a wooden spoon. And then, without breaking the piece, he would fashion a link for every year of the engagement. When, or if, the match was finally made, he would finish the chain with another spoon to symbolise their undying union.

Above the roaring log fire in the Fox and Hounds at Ainthorpe, near Danby, there are a pair of marriage spoons carved about fifty years ago. The chain has twelve links. It is believed there are several more lying discarded and unfinished in attics and cellars, well seasoned memorials to romances that failed to withstand the strain of waiting. And it is said that an elderly swain in a Dale not far away from the Fox and Hounds is rheumatically carving one today. If so, there will be nearly twenty links in the chain. This plaintive custom seems to be peculiar to the Eastern Dales, and one theory says the idea was imported from Scandinavia. If so, it must be the only contribution the sea was allowed to make to the life of these parts.

Mary leads such an enclosed and totally involved life that the chances of her ever meeting a young man in a situation where a romance could develop appeared very limited. But one day when she was twenty-two, a muscular young man with a monkish haircut and hands like shovels, strode down the lane to Girrick. Jim Smith had come to work at Low Farm, which adjoins the Sunley spread.

For fully a year, they ignored each other. Then one evening, Jim looked up and saw Mary silhoutted against a ridge, leading a Cleveland Bay and its foal. And one hand began to shake

Above: **The Sunleys with some of Joe's innumerable awards.**
Opposite, top: **Mary Sunley at the Great Yorkshire Show in 1959 with gelding 'Emeralda'.**
Opposite, bottom: **Father and daughter.**

Mary Sunley and Jim Smith — and Joe and Connie Sunley.

. . . and then the other. He could not stop them shaking.

A year later they became engaged. He wanted to get married almost straight away, but Mary said: 'No . . . wait'. In 1974, almost three years after that thunderbolt evening when Jim lost his heart, they were still waiting. She aged twenty-one, he thirty-one.

The story of their love affair and their agonising situation is the very stuff of poetry. Despite his years and apparent worldliness, Jim had never been out with a girl alone in his life until he courted Mary. As you would expect, he was the first suitor ever to enter Mary's life.

Jim was not consciously seeking an end to his celibate state that evening he watched Mary walk with the horses.

'I wondered what the devil was up with me at the time. My arm started jumping and twitching — it's a good job no one was around to see me. Then I couldn't sleep — I never slept for a week because I couldn't get her off my mind. A couple of days later when I was ploughing I noticed the hydraulics oil was getting low so I went to get a gallon can to fill it up.

'Instead of going back to the tractor I went to the pig sty and was about to pour it into the trough when I stopped myself. The poor pig was jumping up for an extra feed and I thought "What the hell am I doing here?" And when I did get back to the tractor it took me half an hour to find the place to put the oil in, although it was where it had always been. Thinking of Mary all the time I was. I reckoned it was time I was seeing the doctor, but I didn't dare because he would have laughed at me. Next day I started milking and I carried the first bucket away to the dairy, but went straight past and finished up in the pig house again with the sow jumping up for another extra feed. So I thought that day — it's no good, it's got the best of me. I must do something about it.

'That night I went straight up to their farm. I saw her mum and dad and asked for Mary and they told me she was milking. I went into the byre and found her hiding under a cow, but she stuck her head out and smiled at me before ducking away again. So I waited until they'd finished milking — I hung about for a good hour or more. Then outside their back door I asked her to go out with me. She seemed hardly struck, and just said "Well, if you like . . . I don't mind . . . as long as I can get my milking done before we go out".

'That first night we went playing bowls in Middlesbrough and she was as quiet as a lamb. I was frightened to say a word wrong. It was like handling delicate china.'

But before long Mary was in love, too. The hugely happy Jim wanted to shout it aloud but she restrained him. They must wait 'at least a year' before the bethrothal. This new shatteringly sudden turn of events had to be considered carefully in the light of her situation, and there had been nothing in her life to prepare her for dealing with it. It must have been her turn for sleepless nights.

Her father's farm had filled her life to the exclusion of all else since she could remember. At the amazingly early age of three she had begun to work in the cowshed, her infant fingers doing their best to squeeze the milk out of the udders. She was above five when her father had donned his stern new beliefs and there were no more birthdays or Christmases in the house to relieve the ceaseless toil.

When schooldays arrived, she had jobs to do before she started the long walk up the lane, and there were more on her return. Her affection was given to the animals for she did not find it easy to make friends, although she struck up a relationship with two girls she sat next to at school. But they never came to play on the farm, and when schooldays finished so did the friendship. However, she knows and loves all the animals on the farm, including the cows, and can reel off their names instantly — Sapphire, Starlight, Willow, Candy, Cindy, Goldie and so on — and

Mary Sunley at work on Grange Farm.

remembers with clear affection a Shetland pony called Wendy which her father bought for his children when they were young. She does not like to talk about the day it had to be sold to a riding school because they had all grown too big for it. No more does she like to talk about the time when a cow becomes too old to be of any further use and the knacker comes to take it away.

She admits she had no real friends outside the family until Jim appeared all hot and bothered in the cow byre that evening, and she declares that she has not missed them.

'You never miss what you've never had,' she says, without a trace of self pity.

Most of the influences that shape other people have passed her by. She had no records to play· or television to dominate her, so the Beatles, John F. Kennedy, the Moon walkers and the three-day week came and went without causing so much as a ripple in her life.

'I don't know anything else but farming, do I? I've no hobbies because I work on the farm full-time and I haven't left it much. I went to stay with an aunt in Leeds once when I was about nine — I found it a very busy place — but that's about all. Oh yes, I did go to Scotland on a day trip once. We all went in the car because my brother wanted to see something but I can't remember where we went. We got up early and did the milking before we set off and again when we got back. That's the only time I've been out of England. I've never been to London and I haven't much desire to go.'

Although she and Jim live and work within fifty yards of each other they do not have as much contact as other couples.

'We go out together about three times a week. But I can't meet Jim until the work's done after nine o'clock so we're not able to go to the pictures or anything like that. I haven't been to the pictures much, but I've watched television at his parents' place. Sometimes we go to a pub but I only drink lime and lemon, and sometimes we go to a dance at one of the village halls.'

Mary does not talk easily and turns to ice if any criticism of her father is implied. She refuses to discuss the relationship. It is equally painful for her to discuss her plans for her future with Jim.

'We'll get married when it's convenient, as soon as the situation changes and makes it possible. I can't just leave, can I?'

It was exactly a year after she and Jim first went out together that Mary agreed to become formally engaged. They went down one Saturday morning to Middlesbrough to pick the ring.

'It was a lovely year, that day,' recalls Jim, quaintly. 'Mary took so long choosing a ring — three hours I think it was — and when we got back the cows were coming down the lane for milking.

'She took the ring home and never said anything. Anyway, after tea and when all the work had been finished I went up there. Mary came straight to me, and then got the ring out — it was still wrapped up in its little box — and showed it to her mum and dad. They didn't say much. I think they were stuck for words. In fact, I don't think her dad said anything at all, but her mum wished us all the best of luck.

'Then we went off to see my parents. Mother was bad in bed at the time, but she was over the moon about it and gave Mary a kiss. It almost made her better there and then. I know that the reception we got at Mary's farm was a lot different but it was more or less expected. It didn't worry me, though, because it was a choice of ours not theirs. It wouldn't have made any difference had they objected to the engagement — it's a thing they will have to like or lump.'

Jim is very much his own man but is understandably wary of Joe Sunley. He believes that Joe should get a milking machine — 'it's just hard work and it takes up so much time which could be spent doing other jobs. Anyway, if he got one Mary and me could get out earlier on a night.

'But we get on all right. We don't argue because I've found out that it just isn't worthwhile

arguing with folks with strong opinions.'

It is a very cautious relationship on both sides. Ask Joe what he thinks of Jim and he replies: 'Why should I pass any remarks about him? He's all right as far as I know. He took to Mary, she took to him. He's her choice. I don't really know the lad. You know, in the old days parents used to pick the marriage partners for their children and I think it was quite a good system. Well, when you've been around a bit you've seen a bit, haven't you? Very often young people rush into marriage and it's not long before they're getting divorced.'

Connie Sunley thinks Jim is a 'very fair, decent man, as much as I've seen of him . . . I don't think he smokes and doesn't drink a lot to my knowledge. They should be happy.' Even Joe, who says that the ideal sort of man for a daughter of his to marry would be 'someone who abides by Bible principles', indicates a general approval of the match. Any reluctance on their part is

Opposite: **Wedding-day picture of Jim Smith and Mary Sunley.**
Above, left: **The Smiths' daughter Diane, aged nine months.**
Above, right: **Diane in December 1986, aged ten.**

clearly due in the main to worries about the vast problems Mary will leave in her wake when she leaves for the altar. Most farmers as old as Joe would settle for semi-retirement, but his wife says with a patience born of a lifetime by his side: 'He won't give in, you know.'

It is doubtful whether Joe has worked out a solution. 'We would have to adjust,' he says, slowly. 'The two of us couldn't milk all those cows. I don't really know what we'll do until we come to it.' He is sure that Mary will come back and help with the work, if at all possible, even when she does get married, although Mary admits any such arrangements would not be popular with Jim. Both Connie and Joe insist that they are not holding Mary back, and Joe repeats the phrase which his father uttered when he went to talk to him about his own long-shelved plans to marry Connie: 'Everyone has their own life to live.'

The decision rests with Mary, and it obviously casts a shadow on her life. It hangs there permanently, except for the three or four times a week when work is behind her and her slight figure is swept into Jim's huge embrace. And they can dream their dreams of a farm of their own and the two children they want, and wander the lanes and fields in rosy oblivion.

To see them come together like this is both a privilege and an emotional strain, for they radiate a desperate joy which would tear the heart of Montagu or Capulet.

Jim's longing for the only girl ever to touch his life has driven him to suggest a move to Scotland or even abroad — anywhere where they can be together. But Mary has sadly turned down every plan. They could consummate their romance in a rent-free, rate-free, completely modernised cottage on one of the big farms a few miles away from Grange Farm, for Jim's agricultural skill is known in the area. But even that is too far for Mary at the moment.

I know we're only forty yards apart,' says Jim with a rare anguish. 'But that's too far at times. I want to see Mary in the morning. And at night. And during the day too. I want to see her all the time. But I can't tell you when we will marry. It's like counting plumstones — this year . . . next year .. . . sometime . . . never.'

Postscript

BUT there was a happy ending.

Mary Sunley and Jim Smith finally married, although Mary loyally worked on for her father, until pregnancy intervened.

Their daughter, Diane, is now on the verge of entering her teenage years. *Tempus Fugit.*

Joe Sunley lived until his 83rd year. After his death in 1988, Connie found a home with Mary, Jim (now a construction worker) and Diane in their stone-built cottage close to Girrick Farm — now run by elder son, Barry, who hopes to acquire the tenancy.

It's a beef farm now, but a couple of Cleveland Bays still grace its pastures.

And there is still no electricity!

Children of Eskdale

JOHN RAW is the eighth of his line to farm the stubborn soil of Eskdale. He was also born into a Cleveland sub-aristocracy too subtle to be readily detected. Like his father before him, he is a kind of yeoman patrician, more of a natural leader of his community than any of the loftily titled men in their proud mansions. His wife, Dorothy, a child of the same land and traditions, seems to have been ordained to help him perpetuate the Raw line. This she has done with a rare beauty, giving him five of the fairest and most fortunate children in this island.

The life that the Raws lead from their farm perched prettily on the edge of the vast sweep of Fryup Dale is so well balanced, healthy and free from most twentieth-century pressures that it is almost impossible to find a rift in the lute. They enjoy all the benefits of progress but have not had to accept any of its disadvantages, or in any way damage their rural harmony. They have enough money to afford a car and a telephone, but not enough to overheat their ambitions or lure them from their natural environment. They enjoy a social life rich in variety and share it with the people with whom they were raised. The five young Raws, ablaze with the lusty joys of living on a farm, have all the sophistication endowed by modern communications and are being educated as well as, if not better than, most city children. But they do not suffer from pollution, motorways, urban claustrophobia, high-rise flats or the screech of industry. And they can go out into the night alone without fear.

The children's essential points of reference remain the same as their father's and those of his father before him. From the commanding heights of his farm, John Raw can overlook the valley which has nourished his ancestors over the centuries. Ajalon House in Fryup Dale has been the mute witness of the life and death, joys and disasters of eight generations of Raws. John Raw and his twin brother, Frank, were born there in 1933. There were six other children.

His father, Frank Raw, a clever and successful farmer, carried much stature in the community. He was appointed by Lord Downe and other landowners to act as their agent, and the Goverment made him an Agricultural Executive Officer during the last war. He was also a probate valuer.

There was no hardship in John Raw's childhood, just hard work and a lot of fun. School was a mile and a quarter across the fields, there was a stable full of horses to ride, a river to swim in and plenty of companionship.

'They were happy days. We didn't stray far from the Dale but we didn't need to because there was such a strong community sense. A lot of the activities such as threshing day, sheep shearing and the like were shared. Everyone used to come and help on those occasions.'

A steam-driven threshing machine toured the area visiting each farm. Frank Raw would buy half a ton of coal for every day he required its services and his sons would steel themselves for days of intense labour.

'It was traditional for a farmer's son to carry water for the machine and they were always given a day off from school for this purpose. That thing swallowed hundreds of gallons and we used to

The Raw family of Lawnsgate Farm, Fryup. John and Dot are in the centre, with their children Susan, Shirley, David, Christine and Alan.

carry buckets literally all day to an old poss tub at the side of it. In the old days when we grew sixteen to twenty acres of corn it used to go on for three days, but later we could do it in one day.

'Sheep shearing days were much more enjoyable. We always clipped the last Saturday in June — by hand — and all the family, neighbours and their wives and children used to come for that. We used to shear all the lambs before dinner, just taking their breast wool off, and do the sheep in the afternoon. We children had to catch the sheep, sometimes three or four hundred of them, and carry away the fleeces. The shearing was done in a cow byre and we had to drive them into the adjoining byre. It was great fun at first because we'd do a bit of sheep riding, falling off and the like. By the middle of the afternoon it became a real labour dragging those sheep around, but you still had it to do.

'Then when it was all over the men used to play quoits and go for a farm walk. That's an old custom which has nearly died out now, but whenever there was an occasion there would be a farm walk to inspect the buildings and the stock. The children would play hide and seek and then cricket with the older youths before going in for a big tea party. I always looked forward to sheep shearing when I was a lad.

'Pig killing was a big day too. The last one I remember was at Ajalon, we killed seventeen pigs. My father was an expert at that, and it was in the days before you had to be licensed to kill a pig. He had a wooden mallet and an iron punch which worked exactly the same way as a humane killer, placing the punch on the pig's head and driving it home with the mallet instead of a cartridge. Then the pig's throat would be cut and blood caught in a trough to be made into black puddings. Whilst this was going on the women would be boiling a large copper full of water for the scalding. Great pride was taken in the copper and it was kept highly polished. The boiling water was poured off over the pig to scald the hair and the skin off before it was dressed, which was another job in which much pride was taken. There would be another big tea and then it was traditional for all the men to play nap for small stakes until a very late hour, and there would be a bit to drink. On some farms they would play right through until daybreak. Myself, I didn't like pig killing very much when I was young probably because of all the blood. I know one of my younger brothers wouldn't go anywhere near, so my father didn't bother us until we were old enough to be useful. Later on, I used to kill my own pigs in exactly the same way. Now we take them down to the slaughterhouse, although I still bring them back home for curing.'

The primitive glory of this kind of rural life, cementing together a community which had thrived for many centuries in the Yorkshire Dales, had its final flourish when John Raw was growing to manhood in the nineteen-forties and 'fifties. Apart from a few tenacious pockets, it is now but a warm memory and the valleys are the poorer for its passing.

There were so many highdays in the young life of John Raw that some of the more widely accepted anniversaries were discarded. Birthdays, for instance.

'They used to come and go without anyone really noticing. I never used to get any presents. Except one, that is. I was walking to school with my sister on one birthday during the war when she offered to carry my gasmask to mark the occasion. That's the only birthday present I can remember getting, when I was young. Mind you, two days after Frank and I became twenty-one my father had his sixtieth birthday, and we cracked a bottle of whisky for that.'

Before and after school John helped milk twelve cows by hand whilst his twin shared the shepherding of around three hundred sheep up on Glaisdale high moor. There were always three pairs of work horses, mainly shires and a stag (young horse) in the stables. Every spring one or two young horses were broken on the Raw spread.

'We had two riding horses as well, one a halfbred Cleveland Bay called Jess and a thoroughbred gelding called Sam. We practically lived on horseback in those days, riding them up to the moor to take feed to the sheep or going errands down to the village. My father rode with the Glaisdale Hunt and always kept a couple of hounds for them.

'I suppose we were well off by local standards. Later on, we even had a car, one of the first in the Dale.'

Three miles across the sheep tracks of the high moor from Ajalon House lies the village of Glaisdale. It was there at Number 10 High Street, on New Year's Day in 1938, as the hounds bayed and hare soup was served to mark the first hunt of the year, that Dorothy was born, the first child of William and Annie Welford.

At that time, William Welford earned a living filling tubs full of hard slag, which were taken away by Surrey County Council to make their roads. The blast furnace for local iron ore which had once flourished at Glaisdale had waned and died with Paddy Waddell's railway, which was supposed to link it with the major industrial centres of the North East, but the legacy of its waste gave work to another generation.

By a strange quirk of nature the slag heaps also gave people an exotic fruit for their tables — wild strawberries. Dot Raw remembers them growing profusely on the arid slopes, and she and her brother and sister used to collect jam jars full of the tiny berries in the summers of their childhood.

Like her husband, Dot has glowing memories of a kind of young life which has now virtually disappeared, when children created their own fun out in the open.

'We played all the old games in the streets of Glaisdale — ball games, hop scotch on the pavement, cowboys and indians. It was quite the thing at weekends for all the mothers to take their children down to Mill Wood for a picnic and we used to swim in the River Esk. It was very clean and safe, as long as we didn't go near a place which had a whirlpool. There had been a few tragedies because of that, I believe. We never had much money, but it didn't matter. We were all well fed and clothed. Occasionally, my father used to take us on the train to Whitby for a treat and there was the annual Sunday School outing to Scarborough. But we didn't go far very often, because we didn't have a car, and we never had a family holiday.'

Dot changed her home several times as a child because her father, the son of a farmer, went back to the land. After taking one or two positions, he settled at Wind Hill, a farm in between Glaisdale and Lealholm.

'I was about thirteen at the time and Wind Hill was bought by a man called Stonehouse, who had been a tea planter in India. He left when the British got out of India, and was the talk of the village because he paid what was then a fantastic price for a ninety-odd acre farm — five thousand pounds. (He was a bachelor at the time and very kind, although he was very remote and rarely mixed with the villagers. He never talked about his past.) He learned how to be a farmer from books and hired my father to help him. The wage included our services too. We lived at one end of the long farmhouse and had to help on the farm and look after him. Mum and I had to cook his meals and keep the house clean, including the dusting of the elephant's tusks and other trophies from India.

'There was always a lot of work — and work came first. I looked after the calves, and I remember getting ring worms from them once, all across my chest. The ironing was always waiting for me when I came home from school on Monday evening.'

When Dot, a bright and extroverted young lady, left school at sixteen, she managed to avoid a shop counter job and found an outlet for her creative ability by persuading photographer Bill Eglin Shaw to hire her. He is now well established in Whitby as the custodian of the world-famous Frank Meadow Sutcliffe plates, which he promotes and markets with energy and flair. At the time Dot joined him he was in a more modest way of business in the village of Loftus, twelve miles away from Wind Hill.

'I had to take lodgings in the village because there was no bus service in the area at the time. That took thirty shillings out of my wages, which were only two pounds. I used to spend most of my time in the dark room doing the printing and finishing and went out with Mr Shaw on weddings and commercial work as his assistant.'

Two or three years before she went to work, Dot had become aware of a farm lad from over the moor with a mass of dark, wavy hair and a permanent grin. He too had cast a reflective eye on the girl with long pigtails known through the dale as 'Little Dot' because she was so small, although she had 'plenty to say for herself'.

The Welfords and the Raws knew each other because Dot's father was known everywhere as 'Warag Willie'. He had an appointment under the war agricultural administration and ran the thresher which attended Ajalon House each year.

'We really met first of all at the cricket matches between Glaisdale and Fryup,' Dot recalls. 'Then he took me home from the Glaisdale village dance — in his car! He was able to cut a real dash in those days because he could borrow his father's car, but on the other hand he couldn't dance and there were fourteen others in the car as well. Then he got called up to do his National Service and he asked me to write to him. It wasn't serious then because I was only fourteen and he was eighteen, but it was quite something to have a soldier's photograph on your dressing-table. I had lots of boyfriends as well.'

Already John Raw stood out from the other young men of the Dale. They turned naturally to him for leadership, as their fathers had turned to his father, and by sixteen he was chairman of the local Young Farmers' Club.

The sons of farmers were almost exclusively exempt from National Service but John, who admits he wanted to go anyway, was trapped by two things: his honesty, and the fact that he was a twin.

'When my brother Frank and I went for an interview he put himself down as a shepherd, which he was, and I put myself down as a stocksman, which was also true because we were a stock-rearing farm. Then this woman sat behind the desk asked casually whether I did anything else but look after the stock, and I said "Oh yes." Well, that did it. She promptly said she would have to classify me as a general farmworker and no arguments, which meant I wasn't exempt. Frank was all right because he worked solely with stock — although there couldn't really have been a farmer's son anywhere who specialised in one job.

'I went in on the day that King George died and we had to be on parade for his funeral three days later. That transformation from being a farm lad to a well-drilled and licked-into-shape soldier on a parade ground was one of the big traumas of my life.

'But then it all changed again and became two years of sheer luxury. I joined the Royal Artillery and my unit was sent to Germany, which I enjoyed very much. Suddenly it dawned on me that there was something else in the world apart from farming and Fryup Dale. I'm afraid I began to like the freedom and the wide horizons of life on the continent. I really took to it. And I began to fear coming back to farming when the time drew near for demob. In fact, I very nearly emigrated to South Africa. I got to know a major who was tied up with gold mining and goodness knows how many other things out there, and he tried very hard to persuade me to go.'

But there was a pull of the diminutive girl now rising sixteen, with the raven hair and large brown eyes, who kept his photograph in her bedroom and wrote romantic letters.

'I don't suppose you could say we were really serious about each other, in spite of those letters', says Dot. 'He used to send me nylons though, sheer black nylons with seams. You just couldn't buy them in England at the time and he used to swap coffee for them. I was the envy of all the girls in the Dale.

'But oh dear, he was terribly unsettled when he first came out of the army. It lasted for a full year. If there was a fight going then he would be in it.'

'Yes, I suppose I was a bit of a lad when I came out of the army,' admits John. 'But I was under quite a bit of strain trying to adjust to living in a Dale again and wondering whether I should get out of farming — out of the country, perhaps. So I used to go around with my pals, having a few pints — not many, because we were still hard up — and looking for a bit of excitement.'

One of the places guaranteed to provide the excitement they craved was the fishing village of Staithes, a steep place full of quaint alleys and crooked houses which looks as though it has been stolen from Cornwall. Generations of youths have clashed along its moonlit harbour and cobbled streets, for Staithes has always been the traditional flashpoint between the two religions of East Cleveland — the sea dwellers and the dalesfolk's. 'Tater-heads' and 'scaly-backs' are the insults traditionally traded between the two factions, and the dalesfolk have sometimes been driven out of Staithes in a shower of fish heads. There is still said to be tension between the two groups in the senior playgrounds in the Whitby area.

Throughout this turbulent period in John's life, Dot never strayed from his side. Gradually, John began to direct more of his energies back into farming but he had no wages or set pocket money. This came hard to a man used to regular pay.

'I never really knew what my wages were. Father used to put them straight into the bank in a lump sum once or twice a year. I had to make most of my pocket money by trapping and shooting rabbits to sell to a man who used to come round the Dale. I'd get a bit of cash sometimes on a Saturday night by getting round my mum but I often had to count coppers to see if I had enough for both a pint and a ticket to the dance. But Dad was very good to me when I came out of the army, allowing me to use the car quite a bit. And then one day he came to me and said: "You had to go away when your brothers stayed at home earning wages so I'm going to give you Sam (the horse). There's quite a keen buyer for him."

Encouraged, John threw himself into the social life of the Dale, hunting with the Glaisdale and becoming chairman of the cricket club (which he remains to this day). Then his father went into hospital for two major operations so he had to shoulder even more responsibility on the farm. At the same time Dot's father had to move to another job on a farm twenty miles away at Nunthorpe, near Middlesbrough. The ex-tea planter had decided to stop farming Wind Hill. But this did not dampen John's ardour.

'He used to come three times a week, Wednesdays, Saturdays, and Sundays,' recalls Dot, fondly. 'Even at haymaking he would turn up. And then I would go and spend weekends at Ajalon. Those were lovely times because John's family made me so welcome.'

'Aye, she was the apple of my father's eye,' says John.

There was one drama which disturbed the tranquillity of their lives, when Dot was taken suddenly and seriously ill with appendicitis at her lodgings in Whitley Bay and permission to operate was urgently required from her parents.

'I got a telephone message at two o'clock one afternoon from the police saying that my fiancée was in Tynemouth Infirmary and could I get her mother there to put her signature on this form, because they couldn't operate without it. By heck, that was the biggest dash I've ever had in my life. I got my father's car and went like a bat out of hell. There was a police escort waiting for me

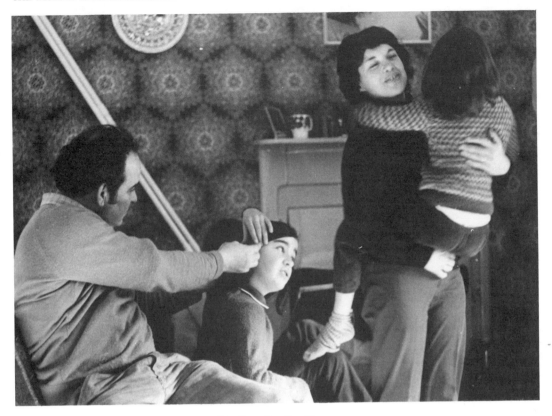

The Raw family at home.

on the outskirts of Newcastle'.

Dot had been struck down during the night in her digs and had not been found until the following day. But she soon recovered.

At the time, John and Dot were officially engaged. On her eighteenth birthday, New Year's Day, 1956, they went to Middlesbrough and chose a ring. Dot's father pontificated a little about her being too young but both he and his wife were privately delighted at the match. There was unreserved joy at Ajalon House. John had no chance to start carving marriage spoons. By the following year they were married.

'We hadn't intended getting wed so soon but the chance of this farm came up in November, 1956. Even in those days it wasn't easy getting a farm to let — the chances were much better than today, of course, but you had no choice. There were only fifty acres but it was a case of grabbing what you could get, so I grabbed.'

The date of the wedding created the only mild friction ever to occur between Dot and John's fond father.

'He said John and I were to get married before lambing time in February, but I put my foot down and said that under no circumstances would I wear a white wedding dress in February. I decided on Easter Monday and he thought it was a ridiculous time for farming folk to marry, which I suppose was true, because it's a very busy period. Traditionally, farmers marry between sowing and harvest — round about May, just before hay making. But I was determined to choose my own wedding day whatever anyone thought.'

A good Dales wedding is a tremendous affair, particularly when it unites two well established families from the same area. It is something to plan and prepare for months, and to remember for years. The wedding of John Raw and Dorothy Welford positively resounded through the valleys of the Esk.

On the great day, each of the myriad moorland roads and winding valley lanes of East Cleveland carried at least one family heading for Glaisdale and Ajalon House to join a motley collection of vehicles which formed into a procession, headed by a hired bus. A splendid progress was then made to the bride's home at Nunthorpe and afterwards to the local parish church. The ceremony had all the trimmings, and if there was ever a truly radiant young bride then it was Dot, just nineteen. She had made her own wedding dress, complete with seventy-five buttons.

Then the feasting began. It was a home-made wedding from the dress downwards. John's father gave a ham, his mother made the cake, Dot's mother cooked and presented a traditional Dales tea, a barrel of ale was skilfully tapped and the walls of Nunthorpe Women's Institute hall bulged with the happiness of the occasion. A group of younger male relatives slipped away to watch Middlesbrough play a match and came back to find the party still going strong. One elderly aunt was outraged because they started drinking whisky out of cups, would you believe!

The world was trembling on the brink of the Suez war at the time . . . well, that other world over the Cleveland Hills was. It would have taken something really serious, like milk fever or foot and mouth, to take the shine off that wedding. Petrol rationing meant that John could not borrow his father's car so they took the train to Edinburgh for their honeymoon, all four blissful days of it. They enjoyed it so much that they booked again — for their silver wedding. They knew even then that it would probably be that long before they would have the chance to go again. People who farm have to make sacrifices.

So John and Dot arrived, bursting with youth and hope, on the doorstep of Lawnsgate Farm, Fryup, to face — total chaos.

'I don't know how any young bride had the guts to make a start in this place,' says John, ruefully. 'For a start, it hadn't been lived in for six months. There was no running water inside, no electricity and the toilet was at the bottom of the field. There was a tap at the back, but if the farmer down below turned his tap on he took all the pressure. And it was in a real shambles. Dot had to work like a slave to get the place right but she loved it, because it was her own place. It's a good job we came when we did because we could never have brought children here as it was, or managed to afford them as we struggled to build up a farm.

'My father was very good to me — he treated all his children very well when they got married. He gave me my wages which had been accumulating over the years — seven hundred pounds, altogether. He also gave me a tractor which was only six months old, a cow, a pig, a henhouse and some tools. But we had to wait over six months before we had running water in the house. And we started the long haul to build up stock, keeping hens, growing corn, doing anything to try and better ourselves. It was a real battle trying to increase stock and affording to live, and we had some bad luck to start with. The first six years we lost a cow every year, which was a very serious matter then.'

Dot's labour of love inside the farmhouse took the best part of two years. 'I had just managed to get the place something like habitable when Shirley was born in 1958. There was still one room I hadn't touched and we still hadn't got a bathroom or indoor sanitation or electricity — we used

Tilley lamps — but it wasn't bad. We had a lot of fun in those early days but what a place it was. We didn't even have fences or gates which made it difficult to stop animals straying. I remember one morning when the man came to collect the milk we were still trying to find the cow!'

Four months after Shirley was born, they were able to afford electricity. The following February, Susan arrived, which made John most anxious to have a son. His wish was gratified two and a half years later when Alan was born. And then came David and Christine. Five in all! As the years rolled by, John Raw's skill and expertise in farming, eight generations deep, built up a fine dairy herd and brought to Lawnsgate Farm a glory it had never known before. By his side all the time, helping him to deliver calves in the middle of the night, straining her muscles with him at haytime, lambing time and through all the crises was Dot. As their family burgeoned around them, John increased his income by securing an agency selling — from home — fertiliser and seed for a Malton firm. And their life blossomed in a way which few families are priviliged to enjoy.

Lawnsgate Farm today vibrates with activity and joy as John and Dot proudly preside over the roar of five young lives, each pursuing a variety of ambitions as well as helping to run the farm.

Mark them well, for the ancient and placid rural system which produced this happy band is threatened with destruction, and we may not see their like again.

Prince

IN THE spring of 1973, a door was opened on the life of the Raw family for all the nation to see. For two weeks a film camera became the eighth member of the family, sitting by them, running alongside them, floating above them but never interfering with the joyous flow of the affairs of Lawnsgate Farm.

'Children of Eskdale' came to the television screen in the purest possible form. No question was asked of the Raws, either on or off the camera, and no word of commentary was spoken. Only a little music added. Anything else would have been an unwarranted intrusion. The effect on the viewing public was profound. They were amazed at what was possible in life, that such beauty and contentment could be achieved in the strident 'seventies. They responded to the programme in such volume, by letter, telephone and through the Press, and pleaded with such persistence to see it again at a time when children could easily watch, that it had to be repeated in the Christmas schedule of 1973.

The ease with which the Raws absorbed a camera into their daily life was never really explained. Perhaps the secret of their lifestyle lies buried there — that they are so complete as a family that nothing can disturb them. Certainly their balance was remarkable, as the documentary baton was passed effortlessly from one to the other. They appeared to cram half a year into the film, but it was an honest reflection of just two weeks of their crowded life — with one special climax.

Separately and together, there was so much life for the Raws to live. Alan, the elder son, as vital and attractive a lad as you will ever meet, was already facing up to some of the crises of life at the age of ten. There were far too many cocks in his flock of pet bantam poultry, and at least one would have to be killed and eaten. His father gently but firmly explained that if Alan was to be a farmer (should the chance arise) then he must accept that animals must come and just as surely must go. Even Gyp, their faithful farm dog, would have to put down soon because he was sixteen. And the lesson sadly but inevitably concluded with Charlie the cock having his neck wrung.

But there were many compensations for Alan and his younger, thoughtful brother, David — the wild fights in the haybarn with its swings and ropes, the hilarious riding of sheep, the uninhibited chases over the hills and wild games in the old quarries; the hunting of rabbits for the stewpot with the help of the silent and sinister ferrets and the pleading for rides on the ponies of their friends.

Alongside them ran the girls, but they had their own, feminine preoccupations. Shirley, the eldest, with her father's cool appraisal of life and a motherly attitude to the mercurial junior, Christine, was concerned with her appearance. The first bra needed buying, and so did that navy-blue eye make-up which made mother cringe. Shirley won that battle, and the one which followed over her bedroom dressing-table. Mother's probings about boyfriends and urgings about not going out of the dance hall were fenced with mocking good humour.

When Dot declared that 'you don't kiss boys — they've got germs', Shirley put back her head

Alan Raw, helping with the filming of 'The Children of Eskdale'.

and pealed with laughter before suddenly shooting back: 'And what did you do when you met Dad at my age?' Which had Dot fighting to retain the initiative. But what a superb relationship it demonstrated between a mother and a daughter about to burst into womanhood.

Both Shirley and her sister Susan, who has her mother's dark hair and flashing eyes, indulge in a whirlwind of out-of-school activity which embraces amateur dramatics, ballet and tap dancing lessons, and the youth club, the quoits team and the following of the Glaisdale Hunt and there is scarcely an hour which is not filled for the Raws.

There was only one flaw in this rural idyll as far as the Raw children were concerned. They did not have their own pony. Everywhere they looked in Eskdale they saw horses, several belonging to their friends who were frequently pressed into lending them. Father Raw was subjected to a subtle and prolonged campaign, and many wide-eyed pleadings. But ponies cost serious money and there was the question of a new tractor to replace the eminently pensionable machine which had been his and Dot's principal wedding present.

'I'll buy you one if I can hunt it by day and milk it at night,' he said, as he parried adroitly.

Then one afternoon, as the young Raws wandered the lanes near Ruth Kitching's land, they were riveted by the sight of a pony pawing the ground at the top of a rolling meadow. And what a pony . . . the very stuff of which their dreams were made. A graceful Palamino called Prince with a flying blond mane, who responded to their greeting by disappearing into a hollow and then wheeling back to crest the ridge theatrically at full gallop. Five young hearts were lost forever. With many soft cooings and blandishments they entered his field and tried to tempt him near with offerings of lush grass, but he danced teasingly around them and only Alan's fingertips made fleeting contact with his shining coat. From that moment on, Prince filled their thoughts and they spent wistful hours leaning over the gate to his field. It was a gallery to which Prince loved to play.

All their yearning did not pass unnoticed in this friendly Dale and it was not long before John Raw was told about his children's enslavement. He also heard that Prince might be for sale. Quietly, he went to see him . . . and realised the inevitability of the situation. John's decision was made and then ratified by Dot over coffee in the kitchen whilst the children were at school. Dot did play a somewhat unconvincing Devil's Advocate at first. 'What about the new tractor?' she asked, but she could scarcely contain her excitement at the thought of the joy it would bring to her brood.

'The tractor will have to wait. Anyway I know where I can pick up a good secondhand one. But I've made up my mind . . . and he's a beauty.'

John and Dot agreed that Prince should come as a surprise. The following evening found John in Prince's field, spitting on the palm of his hand and slapping the palm of the owner. The deal was struck . . . and John, grinning hugely at the prospect of what was to come, led Prince away down the Dale to Ruth Kitching's stables. Ruth had earlier agreed to hide Prince away for the night.

The next day dawned brightly. It was half-term holiday and Dot took the children in the car to see John's mother, leaving Dad behind to 'catch up with some work'. Prince was brought and tethered in the field at the back of Lawnsgate Farm. Then John went inside, brewed coffee and awaited the return of the children. They came in at the front of the farm, which meant that Prince was obscured from their view. The entire family sat round the table, drinking their coffee when

Opposite: **Father and son return from a hunting trip.**

John said: 'Alan, just nip outside for me, will you? There's a bit of bant on the back wall that I want.'

Alan dashed outside, reached for the bant — and saw Prince. The moment was unforgettable. For a split second he was paralysed, then he turned and burst into the house yelling: 'Dad . . . Dad! What's that horse doing outside?' In his excitement he had not spotted that it was Prince. John Raw managed to speak seven words — 'Well, I've bought you a horse and . . .' before the room exploded. A chair went flying as five children came out of the house like buckshot from a gun.

'It's Prince!' screamed Alan, as the realisation dawned.

'Dad, how did you know about Prince?'

The rest of the children of Eskdale were capable only of strangled noises as their pace slowed to a trance-like walk, hands outstretched towards this golden vision, as though they feared he

Above: **Prince, surrounded by the entire Raw family.**
Opposite: **Alan Raw and Prince.**

might melt away like a mirage. Even when John picked up little Christine and gingerly placed her on Prince's back, she gurgled: 'Dad, is it really true . . .?'

'Yes, love, it *is* true,' he replied as he turned to place his arm round his wife, whose eyes were brimming with tears of happiness.

And there followed such a communion of family joy, such a celebration of an enviable life that all those who were privileged to share it were swept along by its pure emotion. Many millions did share it, for two hidden cameras recorded every moment. One was built into a dry-stone wall, another shielded by bales of hay. Not for a second did the children suspect they were being filmed.

That scene became the final sequence of 'The Children of Eskdale' and it inevitably helped to release a rush of interest in the Raw family. Their mail was prodigious and scores of people sought them out. One family from the south spent an entire week's holiday trying to find them, starting in Eskdale, Scotland, progressing to Eskdale, Cumberland, before success came to them in East Cleveland on their last day. All were received with friendship, even those who stood down the lane peering at the farm through binoculars. And when the tide receded, the Raw family carried on with their lives unchanged and unchanging. As for Prince, he quickly became the best exercised pony east of the Clevland Hills, as well as the best loved.

Making the film was a remarkable experience for the Yorkshire Television crew. They were enveloped by the warmth of the Raws and lasting relationships were forged. The children's birthdays are remembered, letters and cards sent from exotic film locations abroad and families brought to eat Dot's justly famous apple pie and curd tarts, and to stroke Prince.

Each one seemed to leave a little part of themselves behind at Lawnsgate Farm when the fortnight's location was over. During one day's filming a charge-hand electrician, a stern and senior union official, was left on his own with the Raws to rig some lighting. When the others came back he had a pitchfork in his hand and a far-away look in his eyes.

'I've fed the pigs,' he announced, 'and I'll have the mucking out done in a minute. I'd forgotten you lot existed.'

Postscript

SINCE those halycon days, the remarkable Raw family have faced up to a vivid mixture of sadness and happiness. Sufficient, indeed, to warrant a follow-up documentary transmitted in late 1988 entitled *Children of Eskdale — The Sequel*. The programme chronicled the family's progress as the five children grew up.

The first blow came quickly, when Prince, that much loved pony, had to be put down following an accident with a motor cycle. And then, ironically, Alan spent weeks in hospital as surgeons fought—successfully—to save his foot after . . . a motor cycle accident.

All five left to make their way in the world, but Lawnsgate Farm clearly remained the pivot of life and is still presided over by John and Dot. The three girls left the dale to launch very promising careers, but the boys stayed, wedded like their father to the land.

All but Christine, the youngest, have married and grandchildren are starting to arrive. John has been unwell recently and the burden of work at the farm has been shouldered by Alan.

But the Raws still project an overall sense of harmony, warmth and contentment.

A Romany Summer

A Romany Summer

THE first time I ever set eyes on Sir Montague Smith — better known as Cocker to his family and friends — the situation was uncannily symbolic of the difference between his way of life and mine.

There was I, grinding through the low gears of a car, trapped in a stream of metal which stretched all the way back to the holiday coast of Yorkshire. It was hellishly hot. Tarmac oozed into the tyre treads, the sun strobed off dusty windscreens, shirt tails turned into dishcloths and car interiors became increasingly fetid as the procession shuddered along the road south of Malton, which slices through the flat and fertile agricultural lands of the plain of York.

There was plenty of time to study the view over the hedgerows. Cool, emerald fields. Gentle, poplar-studded horizons. Tranquil, spacious, shaded acres, stretching into infinity. That's where I should have been, savouring the sea breezes which swirl across the East Yorkshire Moors — a blessing in high summer — from the North Sea. That's exactly where I had been two hours before, shirt-sleeved and happy, researching a film documentary for Yorkshire Television when the message came via a farm hand. The damned telephone again. Would I go straight back to Leeds. The boss wanted to see me.

And, suddenly, there was Cocker. The boiling column had petulantly advanced another two hundred yards and opened up a view along a narrow lane cutting directly west. It linked to a grassy clearing by the road. A small, sinewy man wearing a flat cap on a mass of uncombed hair was languidly tying a skewbald horse to the hedge. His face was as brown as a chestnut and he wore an odd assortment of clothes. At the time I had no idea who he was. It was to be another two years before I spoke to him. A couple of hundred yards up the lane was a small, bow-shaped Romany caravan. And more coloured horses, dozens of them, roped in lines on both sides of the lane, which had lush verges.

The column bristled with interest. Gaps opened in the line as drivers forgot to close up the space. But Cocker never spared us a glance. We might never have existed. He checked the knot in the rope and strolled off to his caravan. In the distance, a thin column of smoke from a newly lit fire curled lazily into the air. A dishevelled child trotted towards him, and horses changed their grazing ground.

I was transfixed, car rooted to the spot until a horn blasted me back to my world. Despairingly I tried to turn out of the column but it was too late. The oncoming traffic had closed up and my chance had gone. Trapped and cursing, I had to move forward. The boss was waiting, sure, but he would have understood if I had passed up the conference and gone in pursuit of Cocker. He was just as anxious as I was to try and make a film about the life of a genuine Romany — and this man seemed to be just that. As far as we knew, no one had ever managed to get close to a Romany with a film camera. To be the first to do so had almost become an obsession.

Merely to approach a Romany is difficult, sometimes perilous. No one knew that better than I did, because I had been trying for a long time. The long route to my Romany Summer had

started three years before on the moors high above Elland, in the West Riding of Yorkshire. A friend who ran an isolated pub in the area had told me about a gipsy who lived alone in a disused quarry and who once was a genius with horses. At the time I was making short documentaries, nearly all set in the Dales, just for the Yorkshire region, which had been well received. I was eager for more stories. Eventually, I found the quarry, and how glad I was to have a car that time. As I walked towards the caravan, a fierce old man in an ill-fitting and faded suit challenged me. He was clearly irritable. I started to explain that I was from Yorkshire Television when a dog tore round the caravan and made for me. I won the race to the car by inches, and drove shakily away. But in my job gentle persistence nearly always pays, so I asked my friend at the pub to pass a message to him—he had helped the publican with his horses in the past and was friendly to him, at least. 'Aye, I'll try—but yon's a queer 'un,' was the reply.

A week later I made another approach in the wake of the message. This time I stayed by the car and the gipsy remained out of sight behind his caravan. There was a shouted conversation, culminating in a blank refusal on his part to co-operate, on any grounds whatsoever, and a threat to let the dog loose again. I accepted defeat, and departed. It was a bitter disappointment—I had searched over a long period for someone like him, had occasionally heard of gipsies over the next Dale but only ever managed to find traces. The cold embers of a camp fire, horse droppings and circles of closely cropped grass, but never people.

At least the encounter gave me added purpose. Instead of playing at it, chasing shadows over the next horizon, I decided on some hard research. Where could I be sure of meeting gipsies—what about a horse fair? I knew about the legendary Appleby Fair in Westmoreland, but that was almost a year away.

'Well, you might try Lea Gap,' said my publican friend, 'that's where I get my horses, and the kind of folk you want to meet will be there.'

Lea Gap is an ancient fair, which has happened every August on an insignificant strip of land between Leeds and Wakefield for at least the last six hundred years. I turned up early with a film crew and watched as a small squad of fairground people began to erect swings and stalls and put out large balloons and plastic dolls for sale. Purveyors of saddles, bridles and every other kind of equestrian bric-à-brac came next and studiously arranged their wares. Then came the horseboxes, dozens of them, and the air rang with the drumbeats of frustrated animals, hammering the wooden sides of the vehicles in search of freedom. The next wave came without vehicular aid, some pulling traps and wagons, some ridden. By mid morning that strip of land was heaving with people and horseflesh.

Men with the kind of faces artists dream about stood quietly in groups, talking and examining fetlocks and teeth with much concentration. There was a lot of material for us and we filmed assiduously away. But there were no bow-shaped caravans, no one who looked quite as romantic as the man I had seen from that traffic jam. Altogether, the scene was interesting — but not exactly fascinating.

At the entrance to Lea Gap Fair there is a notice. It reads 'In the interest of public safety the running up and down the field of ridden and horse-drawn vehicles is strictly prohibited. Any person contravening this order can be ejected from the premises and refused entry at subsequent fairs. By order, A. Cockayne, Esq.'

If he was there early that day, Mr. Cockayne must have been pleased. His order was being obeyed. But suddenly, around mid morning, Lea Gap Fair changed character. It was as though someone had given a secret signal, or thrown over a switch. One minute horses were being walked quietly about, the next they were thundering up and down the middle of the field. Most

were ridden bareback by youths who leaned back in exaggerated style as though they were having difficulty slowing their mount, to try to emphasize its strength and spirit. Some were careering along in traps. There were several policemen about, but they stayed on the road outside the entrance, watching, directing traffic but markedly keeping a low profile.

It was exciting, very good to film — and distinctly dangerous. Hooves and wheels brushed by the people, mostly locals out for a day's amusement, still streaming into the fair. Inevitably, there was an accident. One horse cannoned into a small blonde child, who hurtled through the air. Its distraught mother picked it up, fortunately only slightly stunned. Instead of apologizing, the owner of the horse glared at the mother — and the look clearly indicated that outsiders had no right to be there. It was a family affair, and only gipsies and travelling folk were welcome.

From that moment violence hung in the air like a Pennine mist. You could almost taste it. No one was talking any more — they were shouting. Every deal for a horse seemed to teeter on the edge of physical confrontation. Buyers and sellers went red in the face as the haggling intensified. The language was appalling.

And then the pubs opened. The one nearest the fairground is the Bull's Head. Traditionally, the landlord applies for an extension, takes up the carpets, removes anything breakable and hopes for the best. Every seat, every square inch of standing room was filled with the sort of customer you don't argue with. A great deal of drinking was done. Outside, the car park was a confusion of horses and traps and men arguing. In the middle of the afternoon, the landlord thankfully closed his doors with a crunch of broken glass. Back on the fairground the atmosphere thickened appreciably. The day was fine and clear but anyone sober enough to notice could feel the impending storm.

I stood on a wagon with the crew, filming a bit more of the running of the horses, now being conducted wildly and with much noise, but concentrating more on watching for incidents. They came sure enough. In a far corner of the field a circle formed and men began running towards it from everywhere. We ran too, lugging the camera and sound gear, trying to elbow our way through. Before we got to within twenty yards of the epicentre we were being deliberately impeded. Blocked, tripped and shoved, we battled on until we came to a wagon close enough to the scene to give us enough elevation to point the camera at what was happening. The gear was hauled up on top of the cab. Two men below, urged on by the crowd, were fighting furiously, stripped to the waist. Blood was streaming down their chests. Scarcely a foot of film had run through the camera when we heard a roar from the side of the wagon. One of the most ferocious men I have ever seen — large, swarthy and with one eye missing — was advancing on us with a horsewhip. It cracked across legs and backs as we slid off on the other side. One member of the crew had the misfortune to slide off on his side and was punched to the ground. The rest of us fought on through the swirling crowd, trying to find another vantage point. The camera was running all the time and two of us flanked the cameraman, trying to protect him, knocking down the hands attempting to block out the lens. Eventually we climbed to the top of a large and unattended horsebox and just managed to film the remnants of what had clearly been a spectacular battle.

Later on I was told it had been a formal affair, arranged between two families. One had insulted the other at a previous fair and trouble had simmered ever since. So a sturdy young man from each side had been nominated, and a mark drawn on the ground. Traditionally, the pair strip off their shirts, fight bare-knuckled and the loser is the one who eventually fails to come up to the mark. We got some good material of the two men being congratulated by their respective families. It seemed to be the done thing to press a cheek to the contestant's face so that the blood smeared on your own flesh. One placed a hat jauntily on his head and offered his swollen face to the circle of admirers. The atmosphere was genial, almost carnival. Honour had clearly been satisfied on both sides. We were fairly happy too. No one had tried to horsewhip us off our position this time. But our euphoria did not last for long. We began to realize that now the fight was over there was a new interest for the crowd. Us. A group of unsmiling gipsies ominously surrounded the horsebox and stared — and waited. A face popped up at the rear of the vehicle. It was one of the junior members of the crew, who clearly had an urgent message. I crawled over.

'I've heard some of that lot down there threatening to do you in and smash the camera,' he said. 'They say you had no right to film a family affair.'

Thoroughly alarmed, I told him to make his way quietly to the fairground entrance, find the police and ask them to escort us out of the place. He crept away. We waited. So did the crowd below. It seemed a long time before my young colleague's head popped up again.

'I asked the inspector like you told me, but all he said was that if you were bloody fool enough to come into something like this with a film crew, you can bloody well get yourselves out.'

It was a bad moment.

There were four of us on top of that horsebox, hugging the best part of fifteen thousand pounds worth of equipment. A fist thumped into the side of the vehicle, sending vibrations through to the seats of our pants. In perfect synchronization, we all glanced over the side. It was a sight to freeze the blood. About twenty grimly silent men with faces carved out of granite glared up at us. No one looked down again. No one spoke. We just sat there, gazing at each other mutely. The minutes went by very slowly — I will never know how many. Eventually, sounds filtered through the haze of fear. In another corner of that turbulent strip of ground some other fracas had started.

I chanced another look over the side. The hostile group had melted away and I saw them in the distance, hurrying towards the new excitement.

'Let's go.'

Shakily, we climbed down and left Lea Gap Fair as quietly and as quickly as possible. We had our film. We knew when we were lucky.

I called the film 'A Family Affair' and set it to the raucous music of Aaron Copeland's 'Rodeo.' It nearly filled a half-hour slot, was repeated several times on the Yorkshire region and eventually filtered out on the full ITV Network, area by area. It was even entered for an award.

To make a film of that length from just one day on location is more than just high productivity, it's amazing. Two weeks is the average time. But wherever we pointed the camera that day, something exciting was happening. This point did not escape the boss, and we discussed endlessly the prospect of making an in-depth film for the full network about a genuine gipsy family. But I had met or seen no one at Lea Gap Fair who might have become the basis for such an enterprise. More time was spent trailing round scrap metal yards in Bradford and council camp sites for travelling folk, but it was all wasted effort. Every promising lead picked up by either myself or the Yorkshire Television research team faded. Other projects, notably a lady called Hannah Hauxwell living a solitary and remarkable life in a remote and virtually abandoned Yorkshire Dale, absorbed all my time and interest. Nevertheless whenever a conference was called to discuss future material and ideas, the desirability of a film about a Romany was usually mentioned — wistfully.

More than a year went by, and many miles of film about rural subjects surged throught the camera. 'Too long a Winter,' 'The Children of Eskdale,' 'Sunley's Daughter, and 'The Dale That Died,' among others were all well received by the public and the critics. The time came to go out on location again to make another batch. Then one morning the telephone rang at home. It was the boss, as crisp and to the point as ever.

'Get out to my house right now. There's a gipsy with a bow-shaped caravan and about thirty coloured horses camped a mile or so down the road.'

At the time, he lived in a small village to the north of York called Tollerton. I arrived the same morning and we drove straight to the spot where the caravan had been sighted, in my car.

And found nothing — again. Except cold ashes, piles of dung, and grass verges crew-cut by the teeth of horses.

He can't be far,' said the boss. 'I know he was here two hours ago — at the most. We'll find him.'

Rural Yorkshire has a complicated network of lanes, mostly narrow. We had a wide choice, but we worked every one that led from that camp site. Comprehensively. They were all empty of Romanies, bow-shaped caravans and horses.

'It's impossible,' said the boss. 'You can't just vanish into thin air with a caravan, about five children and thirty horses in such a short time.'

But they had. Frustrated, we returned to his house and ate a dispirited lunch, discussed other things. Later in the afternoon I drove away, trying to find a short cut to the A1 to make the journey back to my home a little quicker. I lost my way in the maze of lanes, and began driving quickly to try and pick up a signpost which meant something to me.

Rounding a bend at speed, I accelerated down a long, narrow but straight lane — and rushed past a sight which made me stand on my brakes.

A bow-shaped caravan! And coloured horses, tethered all over the place. I overshot fifty yards before the car stopped, and reversed back until I was level with a camp fire. Three children were crouched round it, clad in a remarkable assortment of clothes made a uniform dark grey through long wear and lack of washing. Hostile eyes swivelled in my direction, and a couple of large brindled hounds, every rib showing, loped around the bottom of the hedge. I got out of the car, and walked tentatively towards them. A small, sinewy man appeared from behind the caravan, flat cap on a mass of uncombed hair and skin as brown as a chestnut.

It was the same man I had seen from the traffic jam that hot summer's day two years before! It was all too much. For once, I did not know what to say, just stood there transfixed.

The man eyed me quizzically for what seemed to be a long time. Then he spoke in a guttural but friendly manner.

'What would you be after, gentleman?' he said. 'Are you wanting to buy a hoss?'

I snapped out of the trance, and tried to think quickly. It would clearly be an error to tell him immediately what I really wanted, and one glance at his entourage told me that this was exactly the situation I had been seeking all those years. Pure Romany!

Er, yes, I suppose I am,' I replied — which was true in a way, because one of my daughters had long been campaigning strenuously for a pony of her own.

We walked round the hedgerows together, examining his animals. His eyes glowed as he described each one — I was later to discover that nothing made him more animated or communicative than his brood of horses, most of which looked as though they shared identical parentage. Obviously well-worn phrases poured from his lips — 'best mare in the land, that.' 'I've refused a thousand pounds for this filly,' this 'un can pull a wagon better than any hoss anywhere.'

I said I was interested, but had to think about it, and asked where I could find him again. Clearly, I would have to get to know him much better before I started talking about cameras. He described a route which he said he always travelled, a continuous circle through the lanes, roughly between York and Boroughbridge.

'And you'll always find me at Barnaby Fair at Boroughbridge,' he said. 'Never missed, as long as I can remember.' I asked his name. He seemed to say 'Semantical Smith,' which sounded superbly biblical. I asked him to spell it for me.

'Nay gentleman,' he said, a little resentfully. 'I cannot do that.'

It was a stupid mistake, but a few compliments about the sterling quality of his horses gradually put the warmth back into the atmosphere, and he raised his arm genially as I drove away.

Back at the studios the next day I was jubilant. 'Semantical Smith,' said the boss. 'That's a marvellous name. Get to it. But don't lose him by rushing in.'

As it happened, it took more than a year of careful ingenuity and research before a single frame of film was exposed around Mr. Smith's camp site. His pattern of movement around his rural world was fairly regular, and friendly farmers would always point us in the right direction. We became skilled at finding the Smiths. Every two or three months he was visited either by myself, the boss or Julie O'Hare, a researcher of the first rank. But the right occasion to reveal who we were and what we were after never presented itself. We had to infer that we just happened to be passing by.

Julie O'Hare solved the problem. During her visits the name of a 'Master Lee' was mentioned frequently by Ellie Smith, Semantical's wife, with whom Julie established a friendly and rewarding relationship. From Julie's conversations with Ellie we gleaned most of our information, including the fact that Semantical was called Cocker by everyone, including his children. Master Lee clearly had much influence with the Smith family and was the actual owner of most of the Cockers' horses. Why he trundled them around the lanes of Yorkshire we never satisfactorily established, because he always asserted that he was not rewarded in the financial sense.

'I just love hosses,' he said simply, and with utter conviction.

William Lee is a man of much standing among both Romanies and Travelling Folk, claiming to be descended from the original Lees, one of the oldest and best-known Romany families. There is many a 'genuine Gipsy Rose Lee' telling fortunes at fairgrounds and holiday resorts throughout the land, but to be really genuine they have to be able to prove a direct blood link with the Lee family. The other classic Romany names are Smith and Boswell. William was born forty odd years ago now in a bow-topped caravan but has now adopted the gorgio's way with some gusto, residing in a very superior house in the village of Raskelf, near Easingwold in Yorkshire. It has large gates featuring Romany caravan wheels on either side, Victorian lamp posts in the garden and is garnished overall with coloured fairy lights. William's wife, Vi, also owns the house next door. But he and Vi and their children spend a large part of the year travelling the country in a caravan, albeit a modern affair towed by the internal combustion

engine rather than real horse power. William much prefers life on the road.

Fortunately the Lees were at their house in Raskelf preparing to leave for a long trip in their caravan when Julie O'Hare went to find them. Both William and Vi were amiable and ready to help after Julie described the kind of documentary we had worked on for many years. William, who revealed to us that Semantical was really Sir Montague, promised to go personally and see the Smiths and recommend that they give us the co-operation we needed. Julie was told to call back after a few days.

Those days passed slowly. It was like waiting for a verdict, because now it would be revealed what it was we really wanted from Cocker. I knew enough about gipsies already to realize he might take offence at the necessary deception. But — Julie returned from her next visit to the Lees in triumph:

'He's agreed! William Lee has pulled it off. We can start filming him any time.'

Next morning I arrived on Cocker's camp site, which had been pinpointed by William Lee, in the lanes off the road leading out of York to Hull. There was an ominous moment as I stepped from the car. Cocker was nowhere to be seen, but two young men began walking towards me quickly. One of them exuded menace, and angrily demanded my reason for being there. I told them I wanted to see Cocker, and that Master Lee had arranged for me to come that day. The youth's clear dislike of this particular gorgio was tempered, but only slightly, by the mention of the magic name.

He gestured down the lane, which was inevitably festooned with coloured horses: 'Cocker's down there somewhere,' he said, and disappeared into one of the bow-topped caravans parked on either side of a smouldering camp fire. Wondering what the other caravan was doing there I picked my way along a muddy lane towards a familiar figure in the distance. As ever, Cocker was attending to his horses. Without appearing to spot me, he finished what he was doing and began to walk towards the camp site, head down and hands in pockets.

I knew he must have spotted me and went to meet him with much misgiving. There had certainly been no welcome for me from the other members of the Smith entourage, and Cocker's demeanour was not encouraging. But as he came close his head jerked up and he grinned widely. He even shook my hand when offered. Much relieved, I first of all listened to the problem he had been having with the horses — that was always the surest topic of conversation with Cocker — before bringing up the name of William Lee and the possibility of bringing a film camera to his camp site. He agreed straight away.

My next problem was how to approach the subject of financial reward. Clearly, I could not send him a cheque through the post after the filming was completed. So I decided to try a system of rewarding Cocker and his compatriots with hard cash whenever they completed a successful sequence. The risk was offending their prickly pride, but before I left to start organizing a film unit I produced two five-pound notes and asked Cocker if he would accept a small advance payment as a gesture of good faith on my part. He nodded non-committally and pocketed the money quickly and without a thank you.

Postscript

THE following summer was fraught with peril — and laced with excitement — as a documentary film was painstakingly put together.

Cocker made life exceedingly difficult by alternatively vanishing into thin air and threatening violence for no apparent reason.

But the programme proved highly successful and is still believed to be the only filmed record of the daily life and basic philosophy of a genuine Romany.

Princes of the Plough

Princes of the Plough

GEOFFREY MORTON completely fulfils everyone's original, picture-book concept of a farmer. Invariably dressed in shapeless tweed, much-abused hat, open-neck shirt hanging out of cord breeches, he is a square-rigged, beetle-browed man with hands like shovels and a craggy face whipped red by constant exposure to the elements. Nothing appears to ruffle him; his speech is slow, measured and richly regional, his mind contrastingly quick and astute.

His farm, isolated on the rolling, windswept plains of east Yorkshire at Holme-on-Spalding Moor is an impressionist painting: squat, stone barns and byres, sepia with age and squared-off to form a cobbled courtyard; steaming middens, sweet-smelling haystacks, sprawling sows with insatiable litters, scratching chickens, ill-tempered geese, friendly dogs; and, above all, Shire horses.

Twenty magnificent beasts roam his fields and do all his work, for Geoff Morton will not readily tolerate a tractor on his land. To come to Hasholme Carr Farm for the first time when he is ploughing with a four-in-hand against a backdrop of one of the spectacular winter sunsets for which the area is well known, is a stunning experience.

Over the last decade, Geoff, his Shires and his philosophy have so excited the media that he has become far and away the best-known farmer in Britain. Picture editors of national newspapers and magazines despatch their most artistic photographers at regular intervals, and television film crews have cluttered up his cobbles more times than Geoff can recall. Three full, enormously successful documentaries have been made about his life and horses. The last one, ending with the dramatically difficult birth of a foal, was watched by a rapt audience of many millions and went on to win the Prix Italia (the world's most coveted television award). It was also transmitted, much to Geoff's amusement, on American television — with sub-titles! A sequence of the first documentary, made by Yorkshire Television, was repeated every night for years during the station close-down.

Most people naturally assume Geoff Morton to be an archetypal countryman, wedded to the land since birth. They are wrong. He was born a 'townie,' son of an engineer and seafarer, in the port of Whitby in 1926. When he left school at the age of sixteen, the natural thing to do was to go to sea. His father had, there was a war on and, anyway, job opportunities did not proliferate in Whitby at that time. So he joined the Merchant Navy and for nearly nine years roamed the world, calling at Australia and all the exotic Far East ports, both seaboards of North America, South America, the Caribbean and the Mediterranean. He rose to the position of second mate.

It would also be natural to assume that after so many years and experiences the call of the sea would remain firmly rooted in Geoff Morton for life. Wrong again. The land had first option on his emotions and no amount of seafaring adventures altered that basic fact.

'It's in the blood, I suppose. When I was very young Dad earned a living with horses. I can just remember seeing him working them in the town, going in and out of the stables. My old Uncle John was head horseman on a farm and Dad used to go out and work there, too. But he never got a farm of his own and went back to sea.

'It is hard to say when my own involvement with horses started. It's not a thing that really has a beginning — it just seems to have been there all the time. I know I knocked about on farms all the time during my childhood. My Aunt Nancy used to say that I would walk a mile just to ride a hundred yards in a horse and cart. And she was right.'

Geoff believes that most of his forbears worked the land. Indeed, one of them figures in a rural legend which was still being related in the West Riding of Yorkshire not so long ago.

'Aye, that was my great-great-grandfather. He was a cattle drover, a position of some importance in those days, which was round about a hundred a twenty years ago. He owned and worked with a very clever dog, renowned throughout the county for its ability to herd cattle of all kinds. One day he was on the road with a herd when a man came to see him. He wanted to buy the dog and offered a large sum of money. But great-great-grandfather refused point blank, saying no amount of money would persuade him to sell. During the night, the man came back and stole the dog. Next morning, great-great-grandfather and his friends set off in pursuit. For three days they searched but found no trace of dog or thief. So they gave up all hope of ever finding him again and set off on the road with the cattle again.

But they hadn't gone very far when the dog turned up behind them — and furthermore, he had a flock of sheep with him! Oddly enough, they never did find out who owned the sheep — I suppose they didn't try too hard!'

Throughout his own wanderings Geoff never lost interest or contact with agriculture, reading whatever he could to keep himself informed. Back home on leave he met and fell in love with a girl called Lucy, who happened to live at Holme-on-Spalding Moor, slap in the middle of the east Yorkshire farming belt.

'The war was over so I decided to come ashore for good and get married. It seemed a natural thing to turn to the land. And quite a few smallholdings came up for rent around that time in the Holme-on-Spalding Moor district, so we put in for one. It had about ten acres of ploughing land and it was possible to make a living off a small spread like that then, growing cash crops like sugar beet, carrots, barley and wheat. You couldn't make a start on a place so small now, even if you could find one, because the returns would be too low. Anyway, smallholdings by and large don't exist any more because they have all either been built on or absorbed into bigger farms.

'With being away at sea I had missed seeing the early part of the sweeping mechanization that happened on the land. The last farm I'd had any experience of was run with horses, so I came back still thinking of horses. It never occurred to me at first that there was a choice. Everyone thinks that I did make a deliberate choice to use horses instead of tractors, but I looked at it from the other side, I've always felt that the question "why horses instead of tractors" was really the wrong one. Horses have always seemed the proper thing, the logical thing to me, so I think the right question should be "why tractors instead of horses."

'Anyway, at first I couldn't afford anything of my own, horse or tractor. I had to work for a big farmer on a neighbouring spread during the day and buckle to my own place at nights and weekends. My employer still had a pair of Shire horses then which weren't doing a great deal of work, so he allowed me to use them at weekends. It was good for them as well as handy for me because they needed work to keep fit. That arrangement carried on for a while until I managed to acquire more land which meant I had to give up working for someone else.'

Opposite: **Geoff Morton and Grace.**

Geoff with his Shires.

So, with very few acres but a lot of courage, Geoff and his bride broke free and faced up to the rigours and risks of independent farming. They agreed that their first major capital expenditure item should be — a Shire horse. There were still a few to be found around the area and the time was spring, traditionally the season for farm sales. Geoff trailed round looking for the right horse, making the odd, unsuccessful bid. And then a sale was announced with four horses listed among the livestock.

'One of them was a very fine animal, a nine-year-old grey Shire mare called Violet. I knew as soon as I saw her that she was the one for me and I did well to get her. We still have Violet. She's just over thirty years old now and she doesn't do much, but she is welcome to stay as long as she doesn't become ill and continually in pain. Most Shire horses don't get a chance to live out their full lifespan because they usually develop serious trouble in their feet and legs and have to be put down. But Violet's legs are still sound, and she occasionally does the odd job which seems to keep her in better shape.'

Violet obviously holds a special place in the affections of Geoff Morton — and farmers, particularly Yorkshire farmers, are anything but sentimental about animals (they simply can't

Geoff's son, Andrew, with three grey Shires.

afford to be). But then, she has given him twenty years of honest toil, and at the same time been an outstanding brood mare. Two years ago, one of her grand-daughters gave birth to a grey filly foal. Four generations of Shire horse on the same farm, and all grey, is more than just unusual. Violet and her progeny form the main prop in the argument Geoff has been conducting now for two decades with other farmers and people concerned with agriculture, which is being debated more and more these days: the case of the tractor versus the horse.

Geoff Morton presents his brief with the relaxed assurance of a man who knows that the evidence is beginning to weigh heavily in his favour.

'The basic thing is that horses are breeding their own replacements all the time. All you need is a stock of mares and the cycle is self-perpetuating. Over the years I think I have bought five horses and sold three times that number. These days a good filly foal can go for between three to five hundred guineas, a colt around two hundred, a good four-year-old mare in foal might be worth a thousand or more; and prices are going up all the time. I was lucky in starting my stock when horses were considered redundant and prices were consequently low.

'Now breeding does not interrupt the work flow because a mare can keep going right up to foaling — it's better for her, in fact. I generally give them about a week off after the birth. There is a gap of about two years before the foals are ready for the bigger tasks but they are generally able to do a bit of light work.

'If you use a tractor, you first of all have to find two or three thousand pounds — or even more, these days — to buy it. And who knows how much they will be next year. Then you have to go out and make some money with it to pay for the oil and rubber that it uses and for the mechanic who fixes it when it goes wrong. Not only does it not reproduce itself, after about five or six years, it's finished — just scrap value. But a horse goes on increasing in value until it is seven years old and holds its price for quite a few more years after that. And it is always worth something, however old it is.

'Now a lot of people say that it must cost a great deal to feed twenty horses, but the farm is self-supporting. In the past few years our major source of income — the main cash crop, you might say — has been pigs. About seven hundred a year we have been breeding. So nearly all the produce of the farm, apart from an acreage of potatoes, has been fed to the pigs and the horses. The system works out very well in more ways than one. To begin with, on tractor-powered farms they are striving to grow as much corn as possible, but there is a limit to the amount most land will yield continually. You are forced to put in what are called break crops — oats, root crops or grass. That has created real problems for ordinary farms because the returns are not good. But on this farm it's ideal. The horses eat the break crops and in turn provide manure to help grow the corn in the following year.

'So with horses you are taking money out of one pocket and putting it back in the other — with a bit of interest, if you are lucky. This means you are insulated from economic conditions like rising oil prices and all the other things that inflation brings. There is even a measure of protection against Governments chopping and changing their agricultural policies. But most important of all, as far as finance is concerned, you are not at the mercy of machinery manufacturers and Arab oil sheikhs.'

But Geoff's belief in the benefits of horsepower goes far deeper than mere economics and no one should assume that he runs his farm today as a result of a lucky mixture of accident,

Opposite, top: Andrew (riding) and Geoff bring in the harvest.
Opposite, bottom: Portrait of a square-rigged man.

Geoff and friends.

Geoff brings in the horses to start the day's work.

foresight, eccentricity and native shrewdness. Much as he loves his horses, they are only part of a concept which transcends annual balance sheets, trying to judge markets or weather or any of the other day-to-day details of a farmer's life.

Now ecology is a very fashionable subject and the multitudinous threats to the very nature of this planet engage many of the finest brains in the world. They sit in the Halls of Academe and worry both themselves and every other responsible person about the imbalances created by what people are pleased to call the dynamic progress of man. With their finely-tuned minds and computers as big as haystacks, they view the problems on a global scale. Geoff Morton's formal education ended before he began to shave and he modestly claims that ecology is a subject 'almost too big for peasants like me'. But he admits to being gravely concerned about the disturbing things he sees happening around him, and since he is both keenly observant and a natural philosopher, and daily engaged in the very area where some of the most immediately dangerous abuses against nature are being committed — namely, agriculture — he has become a grassroots ecologist in every sense of the word. His views and conclusions are as valid as anyone's, and in his own, small way he is doing his responsible best to redress the balance on his own land and give an example to others.

Three studies of Geoff with his two Ardennes mares at Holme-on-Spalding Moor.

'With horses, nature imposes the balance. You cannot take out more than you put in. There is more harmony than with a highly-mechanized system where you are increasingly putting a lot more into the land — dangerous things — than you are getting out as an end product. Of course, the work has to be spread out more if you use horses. You cannot allow it to pile up into peaks quite as much. But on the other hand you can keep on working with horses when the weather forces you to quit with a tractor and put it back in the shed. Particularly when you are trying to get the ploughing done in winter.'

Geoff's major argument against the tractor concerns land compaction which he has been doggedly expounding for many years and which has now become widely accepted. When a horse puts a hoof down it compresses a small area of soil as it pulls and then strides over the rest. Tractors continually pound our arable land and when it is wet — and most ploughing is done in winter months — they slide and smear the soil with disastrous consequences in many cases.

'You see, the whole soil structure is destroyed by the continual use of tractors in the wrong conditions. The air channels are damaged, roots cannot get through and neither can moisture, which leads to drainage problems. Consequently you get trouble with trace elements. So what you have to do — why, use more sprays and more chemicals to counteract the trouble. Farmers are being forced on to roundabouts that they cannot get off and it is alarming to watch the extremes to which they are driven.

Geoff with his faithful Shires.

'Now you have to use medicines for the land just as you have to use them for yourself. But there is a world of difference between medicine and drug addiction.

'And I'm sad to say that too much of this nation's agricultural land is addicted to drugs.'

If there is one characteristic shared by all farms which have steadfastly used heavy horses come what may, it is a sense of timelessness. They look, smell and sound like farms should look, smell and sound and are far removed from the proliferating agricultural factories where the nose is assaulted by the latest wonder chemical and the ears ring with the incessant whine of machinery.

Some may dismiss this view as pure romanticism and totally impractical, but the traditional farms do seem to prosper equally as well and the men who run them are certainly more at peace with themselves and their environment. Geoff Morton's spread at Holme-on-Spalding Moor in Yorkshire must be an outstanding example as he moves towards the 1980's with much the same measured tread with which he met the challenges of the sixties.

There is a perpetual cycle at Hasholme Carr Farm which pivots comfortably on his horses, and all Geoff wants to do is improve it — which he accepts must be a very gradual process. Self-sufficiency is his aim so that his farm and family are insulated as much as possible from the vagaries of the outside world. Geoff can even calmly turn hazards into an advantage. Along the

Geoff and his son Andrew do some footwork.

lower parts of his farm there must have been a thick wood some thousands of years ago which was flattened by the strong south-westerly winds, and swallowed up in the peaty soil. This means the land is studded with bog oak, which his plough sometimes hits with disastrous results.

Whenever this happens, Geoff and his sons dig round the ancient, petrified lumps, chain them to one or more of the horses and haul them out; then they are left to dry out for a year.

'It's a very useful source of fuel for us, keeps us warm all winter long; and with the amount of bog oak on my land we won't have to worry about coal or central heating for quite a few years.'

The proportion of Geoff's income derived from horses increases all the time. He has got out of pigs, has not replaced them with cattle and in recent seasons has used his arable land for growing grains and potatoes. The fame that comes with constant exposure on the media brings in a steady stream of quite profitable jobs, displaying his horses at various events around the north. Twice a year he holds an Open Day at his farm, with all his horses harnessed up and demonstrating their ability around his spread, the local farrier at work in the yard and a magnificent steam engine thundering away at corn threshing.

Up to three thousand people turn up and pay admission at his farm-gate! Just the kind of thing to inflame the ambitious of most men, but Geoff appears to have little regard for such temporary phenomena. And he is, no doubt, right to be dismissive. There are much more important things in life than a public image and he knows it better than most.

'I am a reasonably satisfied man. I do have the odd grumble about the weather or the crops but it's a happy kind of life here. Ambitions? Well, not really. Not the sort of thing you could dignify with the title of ambition. Other men yearn to own the Horse of the Year or win the Champion Stallion award at Peterborough — but not me. If I have one small desire, it might be to visit the United States and see them work with the big teams over there.'

If he did, the perfect way for Geoff to go would be by wind-jammer across the Atlantic and by steam car to America's grain belt. For as he says — and there can be no more fitting conclusion to this book:

'I have often felt that a combination of horses and steam and wind gives you all the power you need for anything that is really worth doing.'

Postscript

IT IS totally gratifying to report that nothing has changed.

Geoff Morton's heavy horses still bestride his world like amiable colossi. Twenty-five work his land, sometimes six in a team. There was one very sad day when Violet, inevitably, reached the end at an advanced age.

Grain is now Geoff's main crop, and ecologists will be pleased to learn that an acreage is given over to growing roofing thatch. His sons, Andrew and Mark, now in their thirties, work alongside him and there are seven grandchildren.

In one sense, Hasholme Carr is now a Stately Farm with a spread of new buildings and is open daily to visitors — personally guided tours provided for coach parties.

Even more of Geoff's time is spent working on feature films and television commercials (if you see a heavy horse on the screen, odds-on it belongs to Geoff) and there has been no opportunity to fit in that trip to America.

But the man has not changed in any way . . . fame has not touched his essential character.

He is what you wish every farmer would be.